Reporting/Writing
From Front Row
Seats

Reporting/Writing From Front Row Seats

by Staffers of
The Associated Press

Compiled and edited by
Charles A. Grumich

Project Coordinators
BEN BASSETT, Foreign News Editor
DOUGLAS LOVELACE, New York Bureau Chief

Produced by
JOHN O. KOEHLER, General Executive

SIMON AND SCHUSTER   NEW YORK

All photographs by The Associated Press

All rights reserved
including the right of reproduction
in whole or in part in any form
Text copyright © 1971 by The Associated Press
Published by Simon and Schuster, Children's Book Division
Rockefeller Center, 630 Fifth Avenue
New York, New York 10020
First Printing
SBN 671-65176-5 Trade
SBN 671-65177-3 Library
Library of Congress Catalog Card Number: 70-144775
Manufactured in the United States of America

I would not want to be a newsman at any other time . . . man's aspiration was never higher in reaching for the stars, his material wealth never greater, and his chance for survival in a nuclear age never thinner. And we, in the AP, sit in *front row seats* to report all this. — WES GALLAGHER, General Manager,
in a letter to the AP staff.

Acknowledgments

For their help on this volume, the editor is especially grateful to the authors of the essays; to John O. Koehler, AP General Executive (personnel), who acted as the book producer and eased a lot of problems; to Marcia Weiner of Simon and Schuster, who helped with the editing and made valuable suggestions; to Ben Bassett, AP Foreign News Editor, who maintained liaison with the overseas contributors, read the manuscripts, and enthusiastically supported the project; to Douglas Lovelace, New York Bureau Chief, who inaugurated the writing improvement program, and to Josephine Castagna and Carol Guenther, confidential secretaries, who handled correspondence and manuscripts.

CAG

Contents

INTRODUCTION		15
DON WHITEHEAD	Simplicity Isn't Simple	22
RELMAN MORIN	Sometimes the Story Tells Itself	28
HUGH A. MULLIGAN	Getting the Total Picture	35
JOHN M. HIGHTOWER	Washington: Presidents and Diplomats	42
SAUL PETT	A Feature Writer Defines His Art	49
WILLIAM L. RYAN	Pressure Can Be a Boon	55
WILL GRIMSLEY	Don't Tense Up—Let It Flow	60
HAL BOYLE	The Sedulous Ape and Other Phenomena	66
LYNN HEINZERLING	A Writer Travels Light	74
PETER ARNETT	War and Essential Truths	80
FRANK CORMIER	White House Beat	85
ALTON BLAKESLEE	Science Writing: An Art of Translation	94
HOWARD BENEDICT	Space: Up from Bird Watch Hill	99

JOHN BARBOUR	Science, Environment & Conservation	106
ROBERT BERRELLEZ	The Latin American Beat	112
JULES LOH	Features Without Rhinestones, Please	119
SID MOODY	Serendipity of Feature Writing	124
ARTHUR EVERETT	Trials, Interviews, Crime	131
ARTHUR L. GAVSHON	The Whitehall Story	138
GEORGE W. CORNELL	Updated Religion Reporting	145
JOHN CUNNIFF	Business News	151
FENTON WHEELER	Covering Castro's Cuba	157
JOHN RODERICK	The China Watchers	165
WILLIAM GLOVER	The Beat of Broadway	171
BOB THOMAS	Hollywood	176
ABOUT THE AP	by Rene J. Cappon, *General News Editor*	180

The contributors identified by specialties for which they are best known:

Politics, Wars	*Science*	*Politics, Diplomacy, Analysis*
WHITEHEAD	BLAKESLEE	HIGHTOWER
MORIN	BENEDICT	RYAN
HEINZERLING	BARBOUR	CORMIER
ARNETT	—	GAVSHON
—		RODERICK
		—

Features	*Spanish-Latin America*	*Trials, Interviews*
MULLIGAN	BERRELLEZ	EVERETT
PETT	WHEELER	
LOH	—	
MOODY		
—		

Columnist	*Modern Religion*	*Sports, News Features*
BOYLE	CORNELL	GRIMSLEY
	—	—

	Business News	*Criticism, Interviews*
	CUNNIFF	GLOVER (Broadway)
		THOMAS (Hollywood)

This book was compiled and edited by Charles A. Grumich, who in forty-three years with the AP was a general news reporter, feature sports editor-writer-columnist, New York city editor, war correspondent, diplomatic reporter, chief of the AP staff at the United Nations (1946-50) and Foreign Desk supervising editor in New York and San Francisco. He worked as a foreign correspondent in the Middle East, Africa, Asia and Europe. Grumich was detached from the New York Foreign Desk to coach and edit a writing improvement project for the AP New York bureau that led to the essays produced in this book. The writing project was inaugurated by the New York bureau chief, Douglas Lovelace.

Contributions from individual reporters to the daily stream of news and features add up to a formidable mass of material that must be put into shape and sped on its way in some orderly fashion to the reading and listening public.

The delivery of the finished product to newspapers and broadcasters is the responsibility of the AP editors. How it is done is described at the back of the book by Rene J. (Jack) Cappon, who as General News Editor is in direct charge of the AP news report.

Cappon previously was the AP managing editor, supervising editor of AP Newsfeatures, a staff editor-writer in Baltimore, Kansas City and Germany, and for two years managing editor of the Anchorage (Alaska) *Daily News*. He was born in Vienna, raised in Danbury, Connecticut, and educated at the University of Iowa.

Introduction

This is an all-star collection of essays on the practical art of journalism by prize-winning newsmen who have produced millions of words reporting history day by day. These professionals were asked to probe into themselves, describing how they operate, what they have learned from assignments over the world, how they handle specific situations and what their intellectual and philosophical approaches are in covering the news. They responded enthusiastically, contributing thoughtful, entertaining, uncommonly readable essays on how they develop their thoughts and techniques in their professional pursuits.

Every contributor is a general news reporter/writer as well as a specialist in one or more fields. For example, the movie critic-interviewer-columnist, Bob Thomas, was the first to report the assassination of Senator Robert F. Kennedy because he was helping out on a political campaign story—drawn away from his familiar Hollywood beat by the personalities present. All the other contributors have had similar if less spectacular experiences outside their special fields. They have a common denominator in being experienced newsmen, diverse though they prove themselves to be in method and craftsmanship.

This diversity of approach and technique gives variety to the daily news reports of The Associated Press. The writers understand the prime economy of the reporting/writing process: they absorb fact, personality and scene, plus illuminating sidelights and, through the medium of lucid English, render them for the eye and ear to absorb from printed page and broadcast. Each pursues his task in his own way but to the same end: to inform readers and listeners with accuracy and integrity.

The discipline the job imposes upon them—the compulsion of adhering to facts, the necessity of avoiding and averting panic, rumor and falsification—is the challenge they accept.

With the requirements of his discipline in mind, the newsman devises techniques to meet situations, and when the pat approach and execution don't work, he improvises. He learns to develop elbow room, to maneuver comfortably within the straitjacket of his discipline. A veteran hardly considers himself handicapped by the demand that he write not only what is *true* but also *the truth,* which he learned long ago are not exactly the same thing.

In their essays, the contributors cover a wide range of subject matter and concern. Arthur Gavshon in London notes the value of interaction of sources and tells how they may be manipulated into a readable, coherent, informative story. Don Whitehead says a roomful of reporters given the same set of facts would produce a variety of stories stylistically, but he adds that this doesn't matter as long as each turns up an accurate account. Relman Morin tells when not to get in the way of a story that tells itself. Hugh Mulligan asks himself whether writing can be taught and concludes that maybe it is best self-taught; Mulligan takes copious notes on impressions, observations, conversations—everything. Jules Loh does otherwise. John M. Hightower and others prefer to dictate over the phone to an office typist rather than use the typewriter themselves. Hal Boyle raises the specter, and virtue, of Stevenson's Sedulous Ape. Arthur Everett says don't talk much; listen. To those who argue that there is no difference between a news story and a feature story, Loh says: A news story lets a reader know what happened; a feature tells him what it was

Introduction   *17*

like to have been there. Whatever the distinction may be, a good feature writer invariably is a good news writer and a news writer can shift into feature writing without any major readjustment except perhaps for the sights, the range and the bearing. As for wear and tear on the nerves, Will Grimsley counsels writers not to tense up but to let the words flow; William L. Ryan, on the other hand, allows that intensive pressure can be a boon. It may be significant that Grimsley usually writes about the lighter side of life, such as sports, while Ryan, albeit with an often light touch, burrows around in Kremlinology and foreign affairs.

The experts seem agreed that they should:
1. Interest (or hook) the reader at the outset.
2. Inform him along the way, providing facts he really ought to know.
3. Keep the reader's confidence, answering any questions that arise from the unfolding of facts.
4. Avoid letting him down at the end (see Mulligan page 35).

The ideal of news writing would have as its goal a three-dimensional view of the subject matter on the flat two dimensions of paper.

The contributors were induced to forego modesty and explain how they perform, with the expectation that their discourse, advice, anecdote and general enlightenment would help set a younger generation of aspiring journalists on the way to becoming capable, confident reporter/writers.

Most of the essays were used in a writing improvement project for young members of the AP New York Bureau-City Staff.

The authors include all seven AP Special Correspondents (alphabetically): Will Grimsley, John M. Hightower, Relman Morin, Hugh A. Mulligan, Saul Pett, William L. Ryan and Don Whitehead.

Pulitzer Prize winners among the writers are: Morin and Whitehead (two each), Hightower, Hal Boyle, Lynn Heinzerling and Peter Arnett. (The title Special Correspondent is bestowed sparingly by the AP management on reporter/writers of certain

The winners of five Pulitzer Prizes among them. From left to right, Hal Boyle (one), Don Whitehead and Relman Morin (two each).

excellence and varied experience. Not all AP Special Correspondents are Pulitzer Prize winners, nor are all the AP Pulitzer Prize winners Special Correspondents.)

After reading most of the contributions, Don Whitehead said in a letter to the editor: "It's a funny thing but newspapermen never sit around talking about how they put a story together. We never analyzed or questioned each other on how each of us approached a particular story. We had no rules. But we damned well knew a good story when we saw one. And what you are doing is getting to the guts of writing."

CAG

Reporting/Writing
From Front Row
Seats

After breakfast, the general agreed to go back up Surabachi so that cameramen could get the picture they had missed the day before. He rode in a Chevrolet sedan to the foot of Surabachi and then climbed out to transfer to a jeep for the steep climb up a dusty trail cut out of the side of the hill.

Wilson asked the driver why the change was being made from the sedan to the jeep.

"That hill's too steep for the Chevrolet to make it," the driver said.

"Are you sure?" Wilson asked.

"I'm damned sure, sir," the youth replied.

Later, the driver was told that he had been talking to the next Secretary of Defense (Charles E. Wilson), the man whose company makes Chevrolets.

"Oh, lordy," he exclaimed. "I put my foot in my mouth, didn't I?"

He was assured he had—both feet.

From The Great Deception: *Published in AP newspapers as a 3,500-word diary on the pre-inaugural visit of Gen. Dwight D. Eisenhower to the Korean warfront after he was elected President in November, 1952, this article won Don Whitehead his second Pulitzer prize. The title refers to the elaborate security set up to protect Eisenhower as he fulfilled his election campaign promise to go to Korea and to the top secrecy maintained by the news correspondents with him until security was lifted.*

DON WHITEHEAD, the first AP Special Correspondent and winner of two Pulitzer Prizes, worked around the world as a reporter, war correspondent, feature writer and news bureau chief and was a political writer-analyst in and out of Washington before he settled down to writing books, with home base beside a lake in eastern Tennessee. His best known book is *The FBI Story,* a best seller which was made into a successful movie and which won him a Freedom Foundation Award. Combat reporting in World War II won him the Medal of Freedom in 1945. His first Pulitzer, awarded in 1951, was for reporting the Korean War and his second was for coverage of General Dwight D. Eisenhower's trip to the Korean war fronts as President-elect in 1952. Whitehead's latest book is titled *Attack on Terror: The FBI Against the Ku Klux Klan in Mississippi.*

Simplicity Isn't Simple

BY DON WHITEHEAD

The telephone call to my home near Concord, Tennessee, came from an old friend in New York with whom I had worked in the same news vineyards for twenty-one years.

"Will you write me a piece on how to report and write a news story?" he asked.

"Of course," I said.

When I sat myself down before the typewriter I suddenly realized he had asked me to explain something I had never tried to explain before, even to myself. This may sound absurd coming from one who has been a reporter for forty years.

So I now approach the subject with the hope that what I have to say will make sense. (As Adlai Stevenson once said after a flowery introduction by a chairman extolling his greatness as a public speaker: "I can hardly wait to hear what I am going to say myself.")

It is axiomatic that every news story must contain the basic essentials of who, what, when, where, why and how. But the maxim does not tell us how the reporter must arrange those building blocks. And there, for me, is the fascination of putting together a news story.

Simplicity Isn't Simple

A story does not begin to take form when you sit before a typewriter and start writing. The shape and quality of the story are determined in the gathering of the facts that will go into the story. And when I refer to facts I am also referring to what the eye sees, the nose smells, and the ear hears. The environment in which a story takes place often gives substance, meaning and vividness to the bare essentials. Without the ambiance, the who-what-when-where-why-how facts in themselves are rarely enough.

A news story quite often becomes a series of scenes not unlike the scenes played on the stage of a theater. This is particularly true of action stories: a fire, a Fifth Avenue parade, a murder, a rocket launching, a battle, a riot, the pomp and pageantry of a presidential inauguration, et cetera. The reporter must take the visual drama and distill it into words that will make the reader see in his mind's eye the movement, the color, the people and the things observed by the reporter. In the Korean war of the early 1950s, for example, I joined a heavy weapons company of Marines who assembled before dawn and then crowded into amtracs (armored amphibious tractors) to cross the Han River and launch an assault on the enemy holding the capital city of Seoul.

As the mechanical monsters lumbered into the river and began moving into enemy fire, I noticed a huge, ham-handed Marine sergeant carrying a carbine in one arm and a cardboard box in the other. I asked him what was in the box. He opened the lid to show me three small, furry rabbits. "They're the company mascots," the sergeant said. "They go where we go."

The amtracs made it across the river and across the fields to the base of a small hill. The steel doors were lowered and the Marines dashed out into a skirmish line. The enemy was firing from foxholes on the hill above. The rifles crackled like firecrackers and there was the tearing sound of machine guns ripping out bursts of fire. I followed the sergeant up the hill and he was still carrying the rabbits.

Then a Korean mother and her two small daughters came walking around the hill—walking through the hail of bullets and somehow escaping injury. The girls were crying, and the mother was

Don Whitehead. A war correspondent writes wherever he finds a perch. Often he draws an audience, this time a waif in World War II.

trying to comfort them as she herded them toward God knows where.

The Marine sergeant saw them and then a strange thing happened. He put down his carbine and walked over to the mother and the two little girls. He took the lid from the box and held it out for the girls to see. They were frightened at first, peering at him from behind their mother's skirt. But curiosity overcame fear and they came to peek into the box.

When they saw the rabbits, the tears stopped. The girls began to giggle. It was as though the battle no longer held any terrors for them. Each took out a rabbit and held it in her hands. Then they placed the bits of fur back in the box, smiled at the sergeant, and followed their mother around the slope of the hill. Soon they were out of sight.

For me, the story of a battle centered on a Marine sergeant, three rabbits, the girls and their mother, and the unlikely meeting on the battlefield. My job was to try to make the reader see, hear and feel the strange scene I had observed. The story broke down into what could be called four scenes. First was the description of the before-dawn assembly of the Marines and the telling of the mission ahead; second was the river crossing and the encounter with the Marine and his rabbits; third came the beginning of the battle at the base of the hill; and the last scene was that of the Marine and the little girls standing on a hillside battlefield looking at the rabbits. Tied together, the scenes told the story of the beginning of the assault on Seoul.

Sometimes I think a good news story is not written but is talked. By that I mean the writing has a conversational quality—as though the reporter were talking to his readers. With this approach the reporter avoids the use of stilted sentences and awkward phrasing. Too many beginners tie themselves in knots trying to write in a journalese style when simple declarative sentences would make their job much easier and more readable. If a story talks well it reads easily and naturally. And if you don't believe this, try reading a good news story aloud. You will find that it flows smoothly past the tongue and the eye.

What is the most difficult part of writing a news story? It is clarity. There is nothing harder than writing a story that leaves the reader with no doubt as to what you are trying to say. After forty years of reporting, I still find myself struggling to achieve clarity. But I know this: it can be done only by simplicity in writing. And simplicity is not easy to come by.

The good newspapermen that I have known have at least one thing in common: they have the ability to stand aside as observers without permitting their emotions and bias to distort their reporting. This involves the old, scuffed-up, badly mauled word *objectivity*.

In recent years we have heard much abuse of objectivity in reporting. There are those who contend that to achieve objectivity is impossible and that every story is subjective, shaped by the writer's own background and prejudices. But objectivity means nothing more or less than fairness. Perhaps total fairness is impossible, but that doesn't mean we should not strive for it.

Organization of a news story is of great importance whether the story is large or small. Some experienced reporters have the ability to organize a story in their minds merely from reading their notes. But my own method—in writing a news story or a book—is to make an outline of the major points of the story and the sequence in which I wish to present them. The story often strays from the outline once I begin writing, but at least the outline points the way to where I want to go and how to get there.

Give the same set of facts to a room full of reporters and each will arrange the facts in a slightly different way. This is not important if the end results are accurate. But assuming accuracy to be achieved in all the stories, then the important differences in them will be the degree of skill used in making the story interesting. This skill is achieved only through experience in writing. There are no shortcuts.

Don't you believe the stories of the star reporter who, day after day, dashed off masterpieces which were rushed from typewriter to composing room to become gems of the newspaper world. I don't say it has never been done. But there has never been a story that could not have been improved by rewriting and by the pencil of a good editor.

And now, back to that problem posed by that friend who phoned from New York asking how to do a news story. I'll be damned if I know.

RELMAN (PAT) MORIN, AP Special Correspondent, won two Pulitzer Prizes and many other honors as reporter, war correspondent, editor and news service administrator on four continents—America, Europe, Africa and Asia. He was AP bureau chief in Tokyo, Paris and Washington, but preferred the reporter/writer roles. His books include *Dwight D. Eisenhowever—A Gauge of Greatness*. Morin was awarded his first Pulitzer in 1951 for Korean war coverage, his second for the 1957 Little Rock school desegregation story.

Sometimes the Story Tells Itself

BY RELMAN MORIN

Ideally, a news story should take the reader to the scene of the action so that he can see and feel and even smell what happened. You do this by piling up pertinent physical details, a facial expression, a tone of voice, a gesture. Generally, it is possible to use color terms, a "bright-red dress," "a blue-and-gold autumn morning," words that help to evoke a visual image in the reader's mind.

To cite an example, I was once writing leads on a trial and the circumstances were such that I could not get enough elbow-room at a seat in the courtroom. Two reporters came and went in relays delivering the testimony to me as their rewrite man in an anteroom. Testimony, of course, was the most important part of the story. Nonetheless, I kept asking questions such as: "How did he look when he answered that question?" "Any reaction by the jury or the audience when he said that?" "How is that woman witness dressed?" "Is it hot in the courtroom?" Physical details to etch the picture.

The following line, in a report of a political meeting, I think gives a picture: A farmer fanned his face with a red bandanna and another, instead of clapping, applauded by snapping his bright green galluses.

Sometimes the Story Tells Itself

My first lesson in the effectiveness of using graphic, concrete details came early, and it was unforgettable.

I was just out of college and working on the *Shanghai Evening Post*. It would be more accurate to say bluffing, for my experience had been limited to reporting high school and college sports for the Los Angeles *Times* and occasionally to writing a small news story. The managing editor of the *Evening Post* quickly spotted my lack. "You've got a lot to learn about this business," he said. "But at least you can write a straight English sentence and that's more than I can say for most of the bums who drift in here."

Perhaps I should explain that the year was 1930. In that era, a newspaperman with an itchy foot could bum his way by easy stages from the West Coast to the Far East, working on newspapers in Honolulu, then Manila or Tokyo, and finally Shanghai. For many such bums, Shanghai was the end of the line. Life was easy and on many different counts it was one of the most fascinating cities in the world. We shall never see its like again.

To return now to The Lesson . . .

One morning the managing editor (who also was the city editor) handed me a slip of paper with an address. "Take a cab and skip out to Frenchtown," he said. "It looks as though somebody wiped out a whole family last night."

Frenchtown was the French concession in the city, a French island in the sea of teeming Chinese, policed by French officers, tough little Vietnamese and tall, brawny browns from Madagascar. Many wealthy Chinese, who feared kidnapers, burglars and assassins, lived there because they felt safer under French protection.

The taxi took me to a large house, obviously the home of one of these rich Chinese families.

A whole family had indeed been murdered in the night along with three Chinese servants, ten persons in all. The killer had beheaded his victims. The bodies were being removed just as I arrived.

A French police captain, speaking English, said he believed the crimes had been committed by a former servant in the household, an assistant cook. He said the master of the house had discharged the cook several days before. The man had protested that some wages were still due him and his employer refused to pay. "There was a row," said the captain. "The other servants beat up the cook and threw him into the street. I think he may be the one."

He pointed out that the killer must have been thoroughly familiar with the house, making his way through a window on the garden and through the darkness to the kitchen. There he took a meat cleaver. Evidently without awakening any of the ten, he went from room to room. There was no evidence of a struggle in any of the rooms.

"If you wish to see the bedrooms," said the captain, "come with me. But it is not a pretty sight." We went from room to bloody room.

When I returned to the office, the managing editor looked at me curiously. He could see of course that I was badly shaken. I outlined the bare facts. He asked a half dozen or so quick questions. The memory was only too vivid. He glanced at the clock. "Now let me give you a piece of advice."

I was rolling a sheet of paper into the typewriter, half-listening. Mentally, I was trying to frame a lead paragraph, something that would encompass the facts and the visual horror in one shattering Grand Canyon sentence. Where were the words strong enough to carry this story?

Then, as though from a distance, I heard the boss say, ". . . don't write this story at all."

I came to with a shock and asked what he meant.

"Don't write it," he said. "Let it tell itself. Tell it as you told it to me, in plain words, the plainer the better. For instance, you said a cop slipped in the blood and fell. Use that. What did he say when he fell?"

"He said, '*Merde.*' "

"Good. Use the quote. Take the customers inside that house and let them see it and smell it." He paused. "Now this is important: Play it low. Give the details but don't try to build them up

Sometimes the Story Tells Itself 31

with adjectives. This story tells itself. It doesn't need anything from you."

In many instances, the reporter is only the amanuensis. The story tells itself.

The most difficult part of writing a news story is organizing it, deciding the order of priorities of the facts in it. Only in a general sense are there any guidelines. In reporting an airplane accident, usually the number of deaths belongs in the first paragraph. But then it may be a matter of editorial judgment whether the suspected cause of the accident, the weather, or some other circumstance comes in the next paragraph.

When a reporter has some time—as in the case of writing a night lead (the wrap-up for morning papers)—he can try to see the story as a whole and marshal the facts accordingly.

Using a terse, one-sentence quote as the second paragraph usually helps pull the story together and give it some punch.

Sometimes, instead of writing the conventional type of lead, you can hook the reader with a narrative-type intro: "Lyndon B. Johnson was hopping mad." The reader is pretty certain to stay with you to find out why.

Visualizing the story as a whole is particularly important when it lends itself to being told more or less chronologically with a beginning, middle and end. The story of the Little Rock school desegregation in 1957 was one such. Once the A-B-C facts were out of the way, I let the story run in narrative sequence: the crowd gathering as the school opened in the morning, the first violence, the entry of the Negro students, the effort to storm the barricade.... One part of the sequence provided its own special dramatic impact:

> *At that instant, the eight Negroes—the three boys and five girls—were crossing the schoolyard toward a side door at the south end of the school. The girls were in bobby sox and the boys were dressed in shirts open at the neck. All were carrying books.*
>
> *They were not running, not even walking fast. They simply*

Relman Morin. At left, Special Correspondent Morin runs with news of a court order requiring Governor Orval Faubus to withdraw National Guard troops from around Little Rock's Central High School in the 1957 desegregation crisis. At right, Morin dictates another installment of his Pulitzer Prize-winning story from a phone booth outside Central High School.

strolled toward the steps, went up and were inside before all but a few of the 200 people at that end of the street knew it.

"They've gone in," a man roared. "Oh, God, the niggers are in the school."

I had to dictate the story from a public phone booth to the AP Little Rock bureau, where a typist took down my words for relay to the general news wires. Dictation is a special knack of the trade developed by reporters who must shoot from the lip, so to speak, to put fast-breaking stories on their way to the general wire heads from which news is fed across the country

Sometimes the Story Tells Itself   33

and around the world. The easiest way, in dictating, is to use the straight declarative sentence: subject, verb, predicate. A more complicated sentence can lead you into trouble.

Finally, I have had occasion to go to the annex of the New York Public Library where old newspapers are kept and read stories that may be fifty or seventy-five years old. It is a memorable experience. It sets me to wondering how something of mine would look in the future, assuming of course it was worth preserving. In the heat of writing a fast-breaking story you can't do this. But, again, when there is time, try to imagine how the story will look to a reader in the twenty-first century. It helps achieve perspective.

AP Special Correspondent HUGH A. MULLIGAN, winner of numerous awards in journalism, is a roving correspondent with London as his base and the Eastern Hemisphere as his beat. Much of his prize-winning prose came out of the Vietnam-Indochina war.

Getting the Total Picture

BY HUGH A. MULLIGAN

Once while dallying with an academic career I taught a class in freshman composition. This was in the days before mass undergraduate unrest, but I did sense some stirrings among the inmates, particularly when they were asked to produce five hundred authentic, original, unplagiarized words.

I never did get locked in the office or have my files rifled by bearded revolutionaries, but the natural teacher-pupil animosities that arise have often made me wonder whether it is really possible to teach anyone to write.

I know one can spend a lifetime learning, because while based in New York I happened to sit directly across from Hal Boyle (essay on page 66) and diagonally across from Saul Pett (essay on page 49) and I was able to observe their gestation periods and vast labor pains. When both were about to give birth at the same time, it was like being chief obstetrician on the great elephant Plain of Serengeti.

I can recall one early and really memorable line of advice on how to proceed in this business of rendering events into words. It was tendered to me by the AP correspondent in Baton Rouge, Louisiana, on my first day at work. He gave me the benefit of his two decades of news service experience in a single sentence.

"Son," he said, "always keep a portable typewriter in the trunk of your car, a ream of paper on the back seat, four sharpened pencils in your left coat pocket, a notebook in the right and fifty dollars in singles in your wallet in case you have to go out of town fast." Reasonable words that I have always tried to follow. . . . The phone rang at 5 A.M. one day.

"Get up to Angola," the boss commanded. "The prisoners have rioted and are holding the warden hostage."

Angola was the state penitentiary. It was my first out-of-town assignment. I grabbed a typewriter, scooped up my wife's writing paper with the buttercup design at the top, borrowed $34 off the landlord downstairs and clattered out to the car. An awful thought transfixed me at the wheel.

I didn't have the slightest idea where the state pen was. I didn't know if it was two miles or two hundred, and I didn't know whether to head up the street or down the street, west across the pocket of a coat), how to get your press card coated with plastic Mississippi River or south toward New Orleans.

It seems to me that most of the advice you get in this business takes in about that much territory. We can learn what sort of notebook is best (I prefer a secretarial pad that fits in the side and fitted with a pin to attach to your trench coat, and the kind of pencil to use. We can learn how to fill out an expense account in a mature, responsible manner, so as not to kill a good thing, and maybe even learn a few good reporting tips, like using the marine telephone when a ship is in trouble and calling the floor nurse instead of the hospital switchboard in trying to get a line on the prime minister's condition.

But when it gets down to the actual writing, most of us, even after all these years, still don't know whether to head up the street or down the street. Whether to start with a quote or an anecdote; whether to begin with something new and then work into the background, or lay down an orderly, chronological tale in the manner of a crime story in the British press, which always starts

Hugh A. Mulligan. He travels the world with notebook and portable typewriter, abetted by a photographic eye and a Gaelic sensitivity to the foibles of mankind. Here, he talks with General William C. Westmoreland, then Commander of U.S. forces in Vietnam, in a helicopter over the war zone.

with the constable and his torch going down the Grosvenor Road and finding a body.

There are no writing cookbooks that can tell you precisely how many quotes and how many statistics and how many anecdotes one must blend and stir to come up with, say, a humorous story compared with an informative piece. There are no recipes on the boxtops of your typewriter ribbons or folders of copy paper detailing the ingredients of a blockbuster or a top front-page piece, and the friendly folk at Berlitz, who can make tourists conversant in Swahili and Thai, have yet to devise a simple phrase book that will facilitate a journalist's passage through a campus riot or a congressional hearing.

On a drowsy June afternoon long ago I got back a college theme from a kindly professor with a two-word quote from

Henry James written across the top as a lesson and a rebuke: "Dramatize. Dramatize."

I think those two words may tell more about the art of writing, especially newspaper writing, than any others I have ever heard.

As news service journalists, we are often, I think, enslaved by the quote syndrome. We tend, at our worst, to think that truth somehow is the sum of the best quips from both sides; that in that middle ground of impartiality, of equal space for all, lies the story. Today in a communications world rendered far more competitive by radio's instant replay, television's on-the-spot camera and the total recall of the tape recorder, the jazzy quote means far less to the reader than the total picture of what is taking place.

For example: A ship is on fire off the Jersey highlands. You are lucky enough to get through a marine call to a distressed ship's officer. The story can and should be more than just his excited or calm quotes. In talking to him, think in terms of dramatizing the event for the readers. Put them there. Make them see the fire, smell it, hear the alarm bells, see the boats being put over the side, feel the heat rising up from the hatches. All the senses, not just hearing what people say, contribute to the total re-creation of the event. Ask the officer what is going on at this moment. What does it smell like? Can you see the flames? Can you feel them? What are the captain and first mate doing? Are there any ships or helicopters in sight? Can you see land? Any excursion or pleasure craft about? The point, of course, is that what the officer says for quote is probably not nearly as interesting as what is going on all around him. Quote journalism, like two lines for the captain, two for the owners and two for the insurance company, might add up to a nice balanced package, but it doesn't make you feel as if you've been on board ship during a fire.

Massive details, dramatically employed, make for a readable story. They also call for massive notes, a trick that I learned when I first went to New York and had the opportunity to work under John O. B. Wallace. John was a great believer in detail, lively detail that made a story move off the page and into your mind and emotions. I thought of him while catching a bit of the

Getting the Total Picture

St. Patrick's Day parade up Fifth Avenue. The drums coming through that canyon of office buildings made an echoing sound that you wouldn't remember later when you sat down to write unless you had written it down in your notebook. There were details that the eye could supply, too, and the nose, as well as the ear. Was there enough breeze to make the flags flap? Was it so cold that the Cardinal had to sit under a blanket on the steps of St. Patrick's Cathedral? Could you smell the flowers just put out in the boxes above the Saks Fifth Avenue awning? When the Irish county societies came by, under those marvelously ornate banners at the tail end of the parade, were there any I.R.A. armbands and how old were the old crocks sporting them? Does the parade still officially begin with a police department whistle and end with a sanitation department sprinkler truck?

John O. B. would want to know all these things and, being an editor, would probably want them all in the first paragraph. He had a theory, which I have long subscribed to, that even the most platitudinous interview, the dullest press conference, can salvage something from the background. Whose picture was on the bureaucrat's desk? What saint's statue was on the windowsill of the Mafia don? Did he have blue eyes, a bulbous nose, five-o'clock shadow? Was there a waiting line of retainers and hangers-on outside the door? The trick is not merely to notice all these things, which we all do, but to put them in your notebook so they will be there when you are ready to write.

I have often found it helpful to copy down emotions, observations, and passing thoughts on how I feel about what I am witnessing or hearing, mainly because I may not ever feel quite that way again and seldom do when I sit down to write, which is a flogging, flaying, frightening emotion all its own. When on a story, even an interview, I take endless notes, probably too many, on everything I see and hear and feel and smell and think and observe and just moon about. Then, I read them over and over and over and over until the awful moment when it is time to insert the typing paper and make with the stand-up words. If nothing else, the exhausting task of reading over really extensive notes provides another valuable procrastination, which may be the thief of time but is the chew-blanket of all reporters.

Given the choice of interview sites, try to see the actor backstage, the detective at the station house, the judge in his chambers, the politician on the stump, the rodeo rider in the corral, not at the bar (unless that's his natural habitat); so if the quotes fail, you at least have seen the subject in his natural surroundings. Above all, avoid hotel rooms. More literary sins have been committed in hotel rooms than any other kind, but the plastic trappings of a Sheraton suite or a Hilton high-rise can sap the sparkle from any interview subject, be he Communist defector or heart transplant survivor, be she go-go dancer or former nun about to marry. This side of the Last Supper, the last big story to come out of a smoke-filled hotel room, involved Warren Harding playing solitaire in Chicago's Blackstone, and even then the smell and see detail about all that smoke survived the best of the quotes.

Finally, I have long been a believer in having a sock end to a story as well as a good lead. In fact, I usually spend more time on the last paragraph than the first in the hope that a truly enticing curtain line will stay the savage hand of the editor in cutting down the edifice of my endeavor. The old inverted pyramid of a news story is dying out, thank God. We no longer have to get all the best stuff at the top and sort of tail off into inconsequentia. A stirring quote, a summing-up anecdote, a funny something to arouse the emotions of the reader one last time, to call up a sob or a laugh, can round off a story so that it appears as an entity, a complete whole.

Good endings are something I learned from the late Barney Krebs, political writer on the *New Orleans Times-Picayune,* who covered the legislature at Baton Rouge in such vast detail every day that his stories often ran thousands of words. Barney had no illusions that the entire *Picayune* readership was following his every word down the lengths of his columns, which were jumped from page to page.

"But I always," he once told me, "save one good quote for the very last paragraph as a reward for the faithful few who've come so far."

As I say, if you find a good quote, end with it.

JOHN M. HIGHTOWER, AP Special Correspondent, has covered politics and diplomacy during the terms of six presidents and nine secretaries of state, and has reported summit meetings wherever they have been held. His dateline from time to time has been London, Moscow, Paris and other foreign capitals as well as Washington, his home base. He won a Pulitzer Prize for coverage of the 1952 Truman-MacArthur collision.

Washington: Presidents and Diplomats

BY JOHN M. HIGHTOWER

The word on the radio one morning was that a new military boss in Pakistan had started his rule with "an iron fist in a velvet glove." I was speeding along the George Washington parkway driving, as they say, 250 horses, and that phrase from the old knightly time of one-man-one-horse sounded oddly out of place in my loudspeaker.

As the broadcast developed the story of the seizure of power in a nation of about 130 million people, it seemed that neither the reporter nor his cliché was very precise. Perhaps his problem was that he didn't know much about his subject and took refuge in a handy generality and a shopworn phrase. The only certainty was that General Agha Mohammad Yahya Khan had deposed President-Field Marshal Mohammad Ayub Khan as chief of state in the world's most populous Moslem country.

I will not join those who count themselves enemies of the cliché. It has been a mainstay of journalism for generations as part of the language of the everyday world which both news writers and news readers understand. There are times when even a dead metaphor is better than no metaphor at all. I simply think the cliché, like any figure of speech, like any word, in fact, should help express and sharpen the idea it is intended to communicate.

Some years ago an editor-critic sent a memorandum to his staff saying we had to put an end to "threadbare clichés." I was never sure whether he meant to leave us the option of using those that are not threadbare. But the value of the cliché to his own creative style was inescapable.

Most criticisms and exhortations about better writing give me a vague and troubled feeling that they are beside the point. They don't tell the writer in need of improvement whatever it is he needs to know. Indeed, no one can tell him all he needs to know; he has to discover it through his own experience. But criticisms can help if they are broadly conceived and not simply negative and restrictive. Improvement campaigns help most if they do not overreach themselves and produce rigidity.

In general, well-constructed short sentences are likely to be clearer than well-constructed long sentences simply because they give the reader less information to comprehend in one lump. But that fact should be taken as a guideline and not a law of divine edict.

Many writers need to practice the simple declarative form. This is particularly true of those of us in the news service business where wire space—at 66 words per minute—has a high value and story length must be kept in bounds. One specific problem is the orphan modifier. This is an idea stuck into a sentence where it doesn't belong, because it doesn't seem to belong anywhere else either.

Suppose there is a story about a college athlete, and the writer wants to include a reference to the fact that he once worked on a pig farm. The writer may not have the space to build this up extensively in colorful language, so he just throws it into a straight news piece: "Abernathy, who once worked on a pig farm, is married and has one child. He plans to turn pro after graduation in June." This kind of confused mixture can be avoided by omitting the secondary information or by stating it separately.

In any story many facts are not dispensable, however. The way they are packed together is one key to clarity. When wordage limitations are very restrictive, one has an impulse to fold as many of these facts as possible into the same sentence. Many of the shorter death stories are written this way. The use of separate sentences for each fact or set of related facts is preferable. The information is more digestible that way, and the word savings achieved by stuffing facts into sentences that are already complete is largely illusory anyway.

Another key to clarity is selection, which is one of the most important acts in the writing process. It leads directly to the central question in all reporting: What is the writer trying to tell his reader? He may be loaded with facts, but if he does not know what he wants to communicate, his facts will prove to be a handicap rather than a resource. Extensive summary stories present serious difficulties in this respect.

A wrapup of campus rioting in eleven different cities, a single general summary on three East-West crises, a presidential news conference covering ten different subjects—all raise essentially the same problem of selection and ordering of facts. But the problem exists to a smaller degree for every story worth printing or airing and it should be recognized for what it requires—a negative as well as a positive action. For every fact included in a story some other fact is likely to be left out; for every fact put high up in a story some other fact must be pushed down.

Stories contain more than facts, of course, even news stories. Notably they contain mood stimulators, which we usually call color, and emotional triggers, which are the color of emotion-charged events. In my view elegant or vivid language is tolerable only if the style of the whole story is elegant or vivid and if the subject is suitable for such treatment.

The approach one chooses for a story not only sets forth its most important or interesting fact but also fixes the tone and limits of what follows. Back in 1944 I handled a piece about the plan put forth by President Roosevelt's Secretary of the Treasury, Henry Morgenthau Jr., for conversion of industrial Germany to a virtually agricultural state after the Second World War. The plan was opposed by Secretary of State Cordell Hull and Secretary of War Henry L. Stimson.

·

Washington: Presidents and Diplomats 45

Inside the government, the situation was tangled up in arguments over the merits of the plan itself and in Washington politics. But there was one simple fact: The Roosevelt cabinet was split over the then most vital of prospective postwar problems. I led the piece with the split as being understandable and interesting. This approach expressed the tone of controversy and allowed me to report both sides of the argument in balance.

I remember going into my office on a Saturday afternoon and writing the story under great pressure so it could make the Sunday morning papers. I paced the writing so that I had to keep up with the beginning paragraphs of my story as they were being sent on the general news wires by a teletype operator. I wound up the last paragraphs almost in a tie race with the operator. Writing under that kind of pressure is better for me than writing at leisure because the story imposes its own discipline. Writing without pressure is harder work.

And for me dictating to a typist rather than typing myself is the easiest way of writing once the technical and psychological problems of dictation are licked. The chief technical problem is advance organization of facts. The psychological problem is a kind of stage fright, a fear of starting to dictate and then failing to think of the next thing to say.

Like many others in Washington, I had to learn to dictate as a result of covering news conferences. A few times when I was alone in the late 1930s I had three or four urgent stories to handle after each Roosevelt news conference, and there was no time to worry about my dictation fears then. Later I found I could dictate over the phone to the office without pressure and thus learned to save much time, even on long explanatory or analytical pieces.

When I have gone abroad I've had to revert to typing and on a few occasions that took special effort, mainly because typing seemed so much slower. In the spring-summer of 1968 in Paris the AP staff covering the Vietnam peace talks used both methods; usually, fragmentary spot reports had to be phoned in from sources around the city while stories splicing all these reports into one coherent roundup were written in the Paris AP office at 21 rue de Berri.

John M. Hightower. Where there's a summit meeting of statesmen on a world crisis, or Washington infighting over American policy — there you'll find Hightower. In Paris, he interviews U.S. Ambassador Averell Harriman when the ambassador was representing the United States at the Vietnam peace talks.

Most big stories of government, politics and diplomacy are produced as a result of situations that develop over fairly long periods. This was true of the principal story that led to the Pulitzer Prize I was given in 1952. During the Korean War, General Douglas MacArthur and President Truman disagreed over MacArthur's effort to spread the war to the bases of the Communist Chinese who had crossed the Yalu River and were fighting beside the Communist North Koreans against United Nations forces. The United States was the UN command instrument and Truman was in fact the commander-in-chief of UN forces and MacArthur's boss. Their differences developed into a kind of feud that produced a whole series of incidents and became a test of the supremacy of civilian authority over military authority. President Truman was determined to limit the war to Korean territory.

As these incidents developed I tried to focus on the fact that each one was part of a pattern arising out of the personalities and positions of the two men. Toward the end of the struggle, I found through inquiries and wrote that the President and the General had reached the breaking point. Three days later Truman fired MacArthur.

Many subjects covered in Washington must be assumed to be unfamiliar to readers over the country, at least in detail. Before the Cuban-Soviet missile crisis developed in 1962, I was asked to do a piece about naval blockades. After I had collected the necessary facts—military, legal and economic—I had a hard time deciding how to present them. Essentially the question was how to interest a reader in a subject remote from his experience and concern.

I finally decided to center the story on the then current situation involving the reported but unconfirmed installation of Soviet missile bases in Cuba. The arms covertly placed in the Cuban countrysides had been brought in Russian ships.

I wrote that President Kennedy had the power to throw a naval blockade around Cuba any time he felt such action was necessary but then explained that a blockade was regarded in international law as an act of war and risks would be high. The body of the story told of the Cuban situation and the history of blockades.

About a month later, having confirmed the presence of nuclear missiles in Cuba, just a lob from Florida, President Kennedy imposed a limited blockade. The approach I happened to use thus proved timely.

SAUL PETT, prize-winning AP Special Correspondent and interviewer extraordinary, has worked on feature assignments around the world and as far offbeat as the South Pole. He has written, edited and co-authored several AP books, including *The Torch is Passed,* on the assassination of President Kennedy, and *Lightning Out of Israel,* on the Six-Day war of June 5-10, 1967. Among the many VIPs Pett interviewed were Herbert Hoover, Harry Truman, General Dwight D. Eisenhower, John F. Kennedy, Lyndon B. Johnson, Richard M. Nixon (in their roles as President, ex-President or political campaigner); General Douglas MacArthur, former Chief Justice Earl Warren, former Vice-President Hubert H. Humphrey, Senators Robert F. and Edward M. Kennedy, Admiral Richard E. Byrd, Dorothy Parker, Dr. Jonas Salk, Dr. Albert Einstein, J. Robert Oppenheimer and former Defense Secretary Robert S. McNamara.

A Feature Writer Defines His Art

BY SAUL PETT

There are no rules about writing I can think of that I don't break —even my own rules. There are no generalizations about writing that are foolproof, except the one I just made. Now let me generalize.

All sermons on writing that inhibit the writer are worse than the sins they are trying to correct. Before it's finished, good writing always involves a sense of discipline, but good writing begins with a sense of freedom, of elbow room, of space; from a challenge to grope and find the heart of the matter, from an invitation to say it differently if the thing needs to be said differently, but never just to be different. Good writing begins with the impetus of one individual, the writer. The good writer does not write for the reader or the boss. He writes for himself. Good writing is self-expression. ("This above all: to thine own self be true. . . .") If you want to get pompous, you can call it integrity. But it is a practical matter. If it isn't self-expressive, it isn't fun, it isn't good, and why not go into another racket and laugh at these poor tormented slobs trying to write?

Good writing is torment and anybody who is ashamed of it, who says that torment isn't professional, who cringes from the word creative as if it were a horrible tag applied only to queers and poets and not to rough, tough newspapermen, is in the wrong century.

Remember how it used to be the mark of a professional to whip through a feature like he was blowing it out of one nostril, march across the street, have a drink and then brag about how he knocked off those five hundred dancing words in fourteen minutes with only three facts to begin with?

Well, we're in another league now, or should be. We can no longer give the reader the fast brush. We can no longer whiz through the files for twenty minutes, grab a cab, spend thirty minutes interviewing our subject, come back to the office, concoct a clever beginning that goes nowhere, drag in fifteen or twenty more paragraphs like tired sausage, sprinkle them with four quotes, pepper them with fourteen scintillating adjectives all synonymous and then draw back and call that an incisive portrait of a human being.

Today the reader wants more. Over his second or third Sunday cup of coffee, he wants to be drawn in by substance. He wants meat on his bones and leaves on his trees. He wants dimension and depth and perspective and completeness and insight and, of course, honesty.

After 500 or 1,500 or 2,500 words, the reader wants to know more about a man's personality than that he is "mild-mannered" or "quiet" or "unassuming." Hell, Willie Sutton, the bank robber, was mild-mannered, quiet, unassuming. So was Dr. Albert Schweitzer.

How can you write about a man without knowing what others have written about him? How can you write about a man without knowing what others think and know of him? How can you write about a man without interviewing him at great length and in great detail and in such a way that he begins to reveal something of himself? How can you interview him that way without planning a good part of your questioning beforehand?

How, when you've collected all you're going to collect, how can you write about a man without thinking long and hard about what you've learned? How can you write about a man simply by telling me what he says without telling me how he says it? How can you write about a man simply by telling me what he is without telling me what he is like or what he'd like to be? How can you write about a man without telling me what he is afraid of, what he wishes he could do over again, what pleases him most, what pleases him least, what illusions were broken, what vague yearning remains? How can you write about a successful man without telling me his failures or about any man without somehow indicating his own view of himself?

How can you write about a man without being there? I don't simply mean being there in the reporting, but being there in the writing. For our purposes, when a huge tree falls in the forest and there is no one to hear it, there is no sound. For our purposes, a story about a man without the writer being in it is a story about no man.

Feature stories without the writer in them are as meaningless as a rimless zero. You cannot capture the feeling of a man without reacting to him. You cannot tell me about him without telling me your reactions and impressions and you can't do that until you think hard and add it all up.

Without a viewpoint, the writer's separate little facts, his quotable quotes, his stubborn statistics, his bouncy biographical data, his clever alliterations, his flashy touches are all so much trivia, strung together without purpose, without shape, without effect.

It makes no difference what you're writing about—a man, a town, a country, an administration, an issue, a team of jugglers, a school of piranha. Put yourself there, buster, and take me with you.

All good stories, all good writing, are but two sides of the same coin. How is this man different from me, how is he like me? Me, me, me. Me, the writer. Me, the reader. Don't just tell me how much the circus midget earns a week. Tell me about his difficulties in living in a world built for taller people like me—how he reaches up to the box to mail a letter, how he makes the high first step of a bus.

Saul Pett. "Feature stories without the writer in them are as meaningless as a rimless zero. . . . Put yourself there, Buster, and take me with you." Special Correspondent Pett takes his own advice at his typewriter.

Give me the extraordinary and give me the ordinary. Does the richest man in the world have everything he wants? Does he bother to look at the prices on a menu at all? That strange, remote, isolated little village way up in the Canadian bush. Don't just tell me about the polar bears and the deer. Tell me, buster, how do they get a suit cleaned there?

A Feature Writer Defines His Art

Tell me the large by telling me the small. Tell me the small by telling me the large. Identify with me, plug into my circuit, come in loud and clear. Don't give me your high-sounding abstractions about foreign aid. Tell me, buster, what this aid's going to cost me? Will it help me sleep better—can I worry less about the big bomb, will it mean, maybe, my son won't be drafted, or at least his son?

And, of course, don't leave me gaping through holes in your story. You know, I think the worst phrase ever developed in the newspaper business is, "Well, write around it." In other words, there's a big hole in our information, let's fudge it, let's throw some grass over it, let's obscure it and quickly get on to the next thing.

Don't tease me unless you can deliver, baby. Don't tell me the situation was dramatic and expect me to take your word for it. Show me how it was dramatic and I'll supply the adjective. You say this character is unpredictable? When? Where? How?

The larger point I'm trying to make is this: The fully dimensional human viewpoint cannot be matched by any machine. The eye of man is still sharper than the eye of a television camera because it is linked to a brain and a heart.

AP Special Correspondent WILLIAM L. RYAN is a foreign news analyst and linguist who reads the airmailed *Pravda* daily, travels the world, and rates as a Kremlinologist with first-hand knowledge of Moscow and other Communist capitals. His books include *The China Cloud* (co-authored with Sam Summerlin) on how Peking got the A-bomb.

Pressure Can Be a Boon

BY WILLIAM L. RYAN

Borrowing from his venerable Chinese forefathers, Mao Tse-tung, the celebrated producer of Thought Books, has told us that "a journey of 10,000 li begins with the first step." This is unassailable logic. Let us, I tell myself, learn from Mao, Confucius and Co. Let us apply their great and profound thoughts to the craft of news writing. Having done this, I have concluded that an essay of 10,000 words begins with the first paragraph. However, while the first step in a journey of 10,000 li is pretty easy to take in almost any circumstances, the first paragraph in a 10,000-word essay can be mind-shattering.

The most difficult thing about news writing is the organization of thoughts. It seems that the more time one has to fiddle around with a story, the harder it is to get it on paper. I have found over the years that pressure, far from being something to fear, is a boon. When the hot breath is on the back of the neck, when the competition is keen and the deadline is the next minute, the story moves and seems almost to organize itself.

The fast-breaking stories—stories of war, strife, turmoil, disaster—often seem to write themselves. But they write themselves more easily if one is familiar in advance with the overall picture.

When I go into a troubled area or a complex situation, I want to know as much as possible about it in advance. There is little time to grope for background when the news is breaking. The background must, if possible, be at the fingertips.

This same rule would apply, also, to assignments such as peace conferences or presidential tours or other such outings. The reporter on the scene must have firmly fixed in mind the most important elements of the story—what it means, the names, the dates and so forth that may be involved—and have a good grip on what has created the situation. One is not allowed much time for searching files. More often than not, there aren't any files where you happen to be.

On the spot story, as it is breaking or about to break, the first thing I ask myself is: What's new and different? What angle hits me the hardest. When I decide, which is usually in a matter of moments, I proceed to hit that hard, to bang out the guts of it, always keeping in mind the need for explanatory words and phrases as I go along. If I am waiting for something to break, I consider various possibilities so that when it comes, I am ready with the outlines of organization and even with an idea of the words I might be using.

But of course, in the business of news writing, much depends upon the type of story, upon the circumstances, upon the degree of pressure or the lack of it, or even upon the reportorial hat I happen to be wearing at the moment. Sometimes the hat belongs to the spot news type, sometimes to the feature writer type, sometimes to the thinker type.

For me, the feature is tougher than the spot news story, largely because with the feature I have time. Unlike Mao's Chinese boy who can charge right out and take that first step, I tend to fuss and fret about that first paragraph. Until I have a satisfactory first paragraph down on paper—one that seems likely to grab the reader—I am getting nowhere. Once the first paragraph is settled, I am on my way and charging.

But *HOW* to write it? How can I answer a question like that? The fact of the matter is, I just sit down and write it. If it's spot

William L. Ryan. The world is the news scope of Bill Ryan, who travels from his New York base to Moscow, Saigon, the Mideast — wherever a major crisis may be brewing or breaking. Here he is shown at the Soviet Liberation Monument in Prague with AP photographer Dieter Endlicher.

news, there aren't many problems. If it's a feature, it sometimes occurs to me that I might be writing a letter to a reasonably intelligent friend. If it's a "thinker," I worry it out. The double-domer is the toughest of all. The writer has the luxury of time, but the luxury itself imposes a further obligation. One wants a rounded, self-contained piece, and one searches for careful organization.

For the "thinker," I find it effective to scrawl the outlines of my ideas with a pen, arranging and rearranging points until they fall into a pattern which seems logical and which satisfies esthetically.

This is a process which, to myself, I call getting rid of the garbage —the excess that would simply tend to complicate matters. I like a double-domer to progress harmoniously from sentence to sentence, paragraph to paragraph, making points and explaining points and documenting points. At the same time I try to arrange the piece so that the reader, rather than being frightened away by the profundity of it all, is lured on from point to point and trapped, if you will, into reading it. The answer here, of course, is simplicity. The simpler you make it, the more readable it is likely to be. This is a real challenge when you are up against complex situations which sometimes seem to defy explanation in simple terms. But when you feel you have done it, you are rewarded with a sense of satisfaction.

Arriving at simplicity in itself is a pretty complex matter. Sometimes, jotting down ideas in advance will help. This doesn't mean writing the whole thing with a pen. I couldn't do that. I'm hardly able to think without a typewriter. It's just the key points I doodle with in advance before approaching the real tool of the trade, the writing machine.

When a story is going the way I want it to go, the clack of the typewriter is soothing music. The louder the better. I'm happiest when I'm pounding the machine so hard that it seems about to smoke and fall apart. It's rough on the equipment, though.

I seldom rewrite once I start on my final draft. Sometimes, in the case of features and long situationers, I find myself rewriting, usually because the long organization doesn't suit me. But I would never hesitate to toss aside hours of labor and start out fresh if the copy failed to satisfy me.

Writing newspaper copy, it often seems to me, requires something akin to an ear for music—not necessarily perfect pitch, but an appreciation of the sound, in this case the sound of the words in one's mind. But a man isn't necessarily born with an ear for words. Writing copy is something that is developed by years of practice and experience, which likely makes for many variations among the practitioners of the craft. You don't learn it so much as you absorb it in a sort of osmosis, and make it part of you.

WILL GRIMSLEY, AP Special Correspondent and triple threat in sports, news and features, has made ten trips to Australia for Davis Cup matches, golf competitions and the 1956 Olympics. Other Olympics and news and feature assignments took him to Helsinki; Stockholm; Rome; Tokyo; Mexico City; Grenoble, France; and many other places. His books include *Golf: Its People, History & Events*.

Don't Tense Up—Let It Flow

BY WILL GRIMSLEY

A few years ago, The Associated Press Sports Department began a campaign against clichés by sending out a note asking sports editors around the country to list the ones they considered most offensive.

An Atlanta sports editor replied: "I'll be darned if I'm going to give the AP my clichés—let them get their own clichés."

Shortly afterward I was discussing the anti-cliché campaign with a group of sports writers driving to a golf club outside Pittsburgh.

"I don't see nothing wrong with them clichés," commented one of the literary geniuses, mocking the anti-cliché campaigners with an anti-grammatical gaffe. Besides, he couldn't see why the word wasn't pronounced clitch, like it looked. This gauche fellow was quickly put right: Cliché (klee-shay') is French for stereotype and commonly means a trite, stale, overworked word or phrase.

Our corn-pone philosopher was partly right, of course. One of the first admonitions given a young writer breaking in on the New York desk under the late Herbert W. Barker, night supervisor, followed the same theme.

"Don't worry about clichés," Barker advised. "People think

and talk in clichés. It's a form of communication—and communication is our business." Barker, mind you, was a choosy man with words who avoided clichés whenever he could.

When I first got into this business I was confused by directives from above.

"Don't be bashful about repeating the word 'said,'" said one directive. "It is better to use 'said' repeatedly than to strain for verbs such as 'asserted,' 'declared,' and 'expounded,' which may not fit the situation."

This was followed some time later by another sheet of instructions which said: "Don't keep using the word 'said' like soldiers marching off to war. Try for some variety."

The young journalist gets a lot of advice on how to write and how not to write stories. Dr. Rudolf Flesch, psychologist and "readability" expert, recommended that sentences should average not more than nineteen words. Yet *The New Yorker* magazine, a symbol of good taste in writing, often uses sentences and paragraphs full of dangling things that run 100 and 150 words, even more.

The best thing to do is read all the advice available, siphon it, decant it, refine it, and write the way that is best for you. Relax. Be comfortable. As a golf pro tells his new pupils: "Don't press. Don't tense up—let it flow."

In years of studying the writing techniques of great reporters and writers I have come to the conclusion that the finest craftsmen have two qualities in common: curiosity and enthusiasm.

You must have curiosity first or you'd never want to get into this business. By curiosity, I mean a desire to know people. What makes them tick? What motivates them?

Enthusiasm is the life blood of sports writing. The best sports writers are those who remain as wide-eyed as sophomores about their work without forgetting that, at the same time, they are observing games played by grown-up men and women in short pants who must be kept in perspective. Often the grim struggles of the players may seem a bit silly when soldiers are dying in battle and people are rioting in city streets. Sports writers afflicted

Will Grimsley. He specializes in big-time sports — golf, tennis, baseball, all the Olympic doings. Above, he interviews New York Yankee manager Ralph Houk.

with the gee-whiz syndrome have been known to write that "courage" had something to do with a golfer's sinking a thirty-foot putt with a lot of money at stake. Guts maybe, courage no.

It is undeniable that the sports pages—regardless of world tensions and the impact of other events, or maybe because of them—are the most widely read section of your paper.

The late columnist Drew Pearson quoted the former Chief

Justice of the United States, Earl Warren, saying: "I read the sports pages first because they record men's achievements. Then I look at the front page because it records men's failures."

Good sports writers are mostly loose and relaxed but they normally hit hard with pungent words and phrases. Sometimes they can reflect life with microcosmic morality tales from their uninhibited realms. Villains as well as heroes abound among the characters they deal with daily and quote with telling effect.

Some of the finest popular writers—Hemingway, Damon Runyan, Quentin Reynolds, Robert Ruark, Paul Gallico—were sports writers en route to becoming novelists.

I have always believed that every young reporter should serve on both the radio and sports desks. On radio, one learns to get to the heart of a story quickly and write for the ear. If you write the way you talk, you have it half made. Sports writing is beneficial because of its wide freedom of expression.

A good story has symmetry. It must have a good beginning. Then it should flow smoothly to be climaxed, if possible, by a kicker ending.

A good writer is like a hypnotist. He gains the reader's attention with an enticing first paragraph and holds his attention until he gets his point across.

The best writers feel a story. If you don't feel it, forget it. The reader won't feel it, either. A sense of humor helps. Keep a lookout for the unusual.

I have enjoyed sports but I have attempted not to be blinded to other interesting events that may be a part of the overall drama. It's wise to keep your eyes open. You never know when an offbeat story will turn up.

Once it happened at Kiev, in the Soviet Ukraine, where I was reporting a U.S.-U.S.S.R. track meet.

I sent out a pair of pants to be cleaned and pressed. Three days went by and the pants were not back. Then five days. Six. Seven. I rechecked with the hotel workers, most of them head-kerchiefed babushkas (grandmother types) like the one who had taken the pants away, nodding "da" to the clean-and-press instructions.

On the reprise the workers seemed flabbergasted.

"Clean and press?" they said through an interpreter.

"Oh, yes, you mean weight lifting."

The hotel staff scurried around looking for the pants. The term "clean and press" confounded everybody. Little groups gathered. I thought a call was going to the Kremlin.

Finally, the hotel promised that if found the pants would be forwarded to the U.S. ambassador in Warsaw. When I got to Moscow I learned the Russians, who could put men in space, had no equipment to dry-clean pants. The pants never turned up in Warsaw or any place I know of, and I assume they had been ruined in washing and thrown away in shame by my babushka.

I thought this was more interesting than the track meet.

While in Adelaide, Australia, in 1968 for the Davis Cup tennis matches, we all were intrigued by a front-page photograph of a dazzling blond girl wearing little more than a two-inch leather belt below the waist and less above. The photo illustrated a controversy raging on beaches at the time.

The authorities ruled that no bikini panties could measure less than two inches on the side. Beach inspectors suddenly took renewed interest in their jobs. The Civil Rights Council intervened, warning inspectors that they would be cited for assault if they measured a bikini on the subject.

Tennis suddenly became secondary. You can't beat 20-20 vision, curiosity and enthusiasm.

As a columnist, HAL BOYLE, the butcher's boy from Kansas City who dreams in poetry but writes in prose, appears five times a week in several hundred American and foreign newspapers. He has covered three wars for The Associated Press, won a Pulitzer Prize, traveled in sixty-six countries, interviewed a thousand celebrities, met a few people he didn't like but never a human being he didn't feel sorry for. In twenty-seven years of columning he has written several million words, some of which he feels even sorrier about. A devotee of the poet Emily Dickinson, he chose a quotation from her as the title for a collection of his columns published by The Associated Press in book form. The title is *Help, Help! Another Day!*

The Sedulous Ape and Other Phenomena

BY HAL BOYLE

The recognition of truth and the clear statement of it are the first duties of an able and honest writer. To find out what really is so and to say it understandably and without distortion may sound easy to do. It isn't.

For words and phrases are bendable things. They can be twisted to serve other purposes than enlightenment. Instead of extending sunshine, they can spread fog and confusion.

But the best and most memorable writing is always built on the bedrock of exactitude.

The problem of good writing doesn't vary whether a man is writing a good novel or a good news story. He must look at the situation, find the kernel of truth he is seeking, and record it in a durable book or in a newspaper which, proverbially, will be used to wrap a fish tomorrow.

Writing is often hard and lonely work, as arduous and wearing as learning to play the piano or to dance ballet. "Wine is the gift of screws," said Emily Dickinson, a superb wordsmith. It is rather like gold mining. Sometimes you must sift a ton of ore to find a profitable ounce of the sought metal.

Some writers with quick minds and fertile vocabularies can swim more easily through words than others. Some, in fact, find the swimming so effortless that they come to admire the ease of the voyage and they forget its purpose—to find a truth and say it tangfully. If not careful, they may wind up writing speeches and textbooks for the Federal government and its politicians.

For those who find the path perilous and the way hard, there is no royal road to excellent writing any more than there is a royal road to learning.

There are a few great writers who achieved their greatness by thinking always and writing seldom. An example might be the classics scholar, A. E. Housman, who coined immortal lyrics in *A Shropshire Lad.* So might be Thomas Gray, the obscure pastor who spent long years polishing and repolishing the stanzas of *Elegy Written in a Country Churchyard.*

Other writers, such as Robert Louis Stevenson, achieved renown by first deliberately imitating a number of other writers until they evolved a style of their own.

Who were Stevenson's exemplars?

"I have thus played the sedulous ape to Hazlitt, to Lamb, to Wordsworth, to Sir Thomas Browne, to Defoe, to Hawthorne, to Montaigne, to Baudelaire and to Obermann," he wrote.

To this list, of course, any number of other writers might be added for their lucidity of style. Among those I would mention are Jonathan Swift, John Dryden—a neglected master, George Bernard Shaw, Robert Frost, G. K. Chesterton, Mark Twain, and E. B. White of *The New Yorker* magazine. But there are many, many others. Our language, if starlit by few geniuses, is lustered by many illustrious abilities.

I suppose that most of us in newspaper writing follow the example of Stevenson. We must plow our path through the clichés of others before we finally learn to avoid them and are able to put words down in a way that is our own. Even then the task of meeting a deadline may not leave us time to polish our rough diamonds and give them the gem luster we'd like them to have. Our craftsmanship is hurt in the hot furnace of hurry, and this can give a conscientious writer an ulcer or drive him to wife-beating and even drink.

It can safely be said, however, that what makes a good writer a good writer is the desire to be a good writer—and working everlastingly at it. The only way to learn to write is by writing, just as the only way a boxer can learn to box is by boxing.

Spending only an hour or two a week at the typewriter is the conduct of a wishful-thinking dilettante. One can never prepare to swim a mile by swimming only twenty-five yards at a stretch now and then.

Many good professional writers make it a rule to write three to four hours or more regularly each day, and perform this chore whether or not the sight of a sheet of blank paper in a typewriter makes them feel physically ill. Any writer who believes he can write only when the spirit moves him is either an amateur or living off a rich wife.

The one sure thing about the muse is that she can be put into harness just like a workhorse and made to plow the necessary furrow until it is finished. Many writers, particularly as they grow older, prefer to write between breakfast and noon, when they feel their minds are at their freshest. But the period varies with the man. Novelist Irwin Shaw in winter likes to start writing in late afternoon, after being refreshed by a few trips down a ski slope in Switzerland. The late John O'Hara, a lifelong night owl, made a habit of writing between midnight and dawn, fueled by pots of black coffee.

Of course, sometimes, a writer cannot choose either the hour or the place of his endeavor. In more than a quarter of a century as a columnist in war and peace I have had to write at every period of the day and night, in the glare of an African desert sun and by candlelight, flashlight and the almost non-light of expiring electric bulbs in small French hotels, employing pencils, pens and Stone-Age typewriters whose ribbons were full of holes. I have written while sitting in trenches, lying on ottomans, huddled in rain-dripping tents, riding in antique airplanes and—once—perched on a U.S. Army latrine seat.

Such experiences do not make one a better writer or a better philosopher. They do confirm a writer's natural tendency to melancholy and paranoia and deepen his conviction that the world was made to enrich his despair. But without this itch of

Hal Boyle. "... sometimes a writer cannot choose either the hour or the place of his endeavor." As a correspondent in three wars, writer Boyle often had to improvise his working places, as outside a dugout, while an admirer looks on.

unhappiness and the certainty that he was born to be persecuted, a writer would probably never be more in life than the historian of a Rotary Club in a small town in Arkansas.

My ivory tower is a cluttered desk in a busy newsroom in Rockefeller Center. I like to get up—if that is the right phrase—at 6 A.M., when New York City is most livable, lonely, lovely and luminous with a gray and rosy beauty. After a ten-minute cab ride to the office, I spend a half hour glancing through the late morning papers and then trudge to my typewriter with the savoir-faire of a prisoner walking the last mile from his death cell.

It usually takes me only twenty-four hours to turn out a column —twenty-two hours spent in nightmares, two hours actually writing it. The question most often asked of a columnist is, "Where in the world do you get all your ideas?" The only sensible answer to this is, "Somewhere between limbo and purgatory, while watching a fly crawl across the ceiling."

Realistically speaking, it isn't getting ideas that bothers a columnist most. As long as he can afford a suit with two pairs of pants and a squeaky swivel chair in which he can wear them shiny, he knows he is in business. Somehow and from somewhere the ideas will come. What he needs most is a friend who will change his typewriter ribbon now and then and the assurance that the *I* key on the typewriter won't break. A columnist with a broken *I* key dwells in a wordless Hades.

It is a harmful legend that most writers dash off their works spontaneously and rarely have to revise them. Lord Byron and William Shakespeare may seldom have blotted out a line or reworked a phrase, but they are only exceptions of genius to the general rule that what makes most good writing readable is endless rewriting.

Only a sloppy writer leaves it up to his editors to improve his careless craftsmanship. The good writer takes such pride in having the right word for the right thought, in paring his prose to a lean perfection, that it makes him bleed inside if an editor finds it necessary to weed it with a blue pencil. I have seen Relman (Pat) Morin (essay on page 28), a two-time Pulitzer Prize winner, tear up a feature story lead eleven times before he was satisfied that he had it right.

And that brings up one of the most vexing woes of the writing trade. A bricklayer knows when he wakes up in the morning that if he has to build a small brick wall by nightfall he can do it—and that he will only have to build it once. A writer has no such self-confidence. No matter how experienced he may be, he is always something of a beginner each time he confronts the typewriter. He is trying to build a different brick wall every time, and so he must avoid duplicating any of the hundreds of brick walls he may have erected in the past.

He may feel like Adam exiled from Eden. But if he works

determinedly at it and conquers his buck fever, by some miracle of practice and perception he has a worthwhile reward; the creation of something uniquely his own. Every life stampmarks its identity and creativity by effort.

The possibilities open to the writer depend to a great extent on his education. Ideally, his education never ends.

Nothing he ever learns about people, ideas or things is ever useless. It is my belief that a writer while in school or college should take basic courses in all the realms of knowledge: literature, history, government, psychology, mathematics, biology, sociology, economics, chemistry, physics, art and music and at least one foreign language.

Then, as a reporter, he will be able to handle almost any general assignment without making a fool of himself. Later, as he matures, he can specialize in the field that interests him most. But he should have a good background before he concentrates his mental firepower.

He should maintain a lively awareness of his times, because if he doesn't, time will pass him by and leave him stranded in a yesterday that daily grows more out of date. Yet as he keeps himself contemporary by reading contemporary sources, he should also seek a balanced perspective by dipping into the works of great writers of the past. This can refresh his own prose style as well as add to his mental health.

Sir William Osler, the famous physician, made this point well in an address to Yale students, "A Way of Life," delivered in 1913:

> "As the soul is dyed by the thoughts, let no day pass without contact with the best literature of the world. Learn to know your Bible, though not perhaps as your fathers did. In forming character and shaping conduct, its touch has still its ancient power.... Fifteen or twenty minutes day by day will give you fellowship with the great minds of the race, and little by little as the years pass you extend your friendship with the immortal dead. They will give you faith in your own day."

Whether or not he achieves a faith in his own day or a skepticism of it, the writer must try to keep up with its promises, challenges, defeats and victories.

A landmark in my own youthful thinking was a small volume titled *What Is News?* written by Gerald Johnson, historian and former editorial writer for the Baltimore *Sun*. He said, "News is what interests a good newspaperman."

That puts a duty on the newspaperman to be interested. The more bored or cynical he is made by people or events, the lesser a newspaperman he becomes. Cynicism is by all odds his greatest occupational hazard. He must keep his curiosity. He must always feel himself another Christopher Columbus or Marco Polo, seeking to find new worlds whether they are bush league or major league.

Since few people ever got rich through newspaper toil alone, is the game worth the candle? That depends on the person and what he wants to do with his time on earth. Its importance is unquestionable. A press that is free to tell the truth is vital to any civilized people, and it is vital to that free press that it employ dedicated men and women who can recognize the truth when they see it—and not be dupes of fraud and hypocrisy.

Yes, journalism is worthwhile enough, but it takes its toll. A study of professional men listed in *Who's Who in America* found that correspondents lived shorter lives than scientists, educators, lawyers, doctors or successful buinessmen.

This was recognized earlier by Horace Greeley, an outstanding nineteenth-century newspaperman.

"Journalism will kill you," he remarked drily, "but it will keep you alive while you're at it."

But what finer way is there for a man to wear out his life than in telling the exciting story of the most exciting century mankind has ever known? He will at least enter Valhalla with no rust on his armor.

LYNN HEINZERLING, an Ohioan, won a Pulitzer Prize for coverage of the murderous conflicts that broke out when the Congo shook free of Belgian rule in 1960. He has reported news events all over Europe and Africa and was in Danzig as an AP correspondent on September 1, 1939, when Hitler's battleship *Schleswig-Holstein* fired the shots opening World War II at the Polish Westerplatte garrison in the mouth of the Vistula. Heinzerling's base is London and his news missions take him around Africa, Europe and the North Atlantic. He concentrated on Africa for years.

A Writer Travels Light

BY LYNN HEINZERLING

One nice thing about news reporting is that the tools are the same wherever you work—a notebook, a pencil, total curiosity, three jiggers of controlled imagination and a portable typewriter.

A plumber who decided to move his seat of operation from Elyria, Ohio, to Europe would need a whole new set of wrenches, new tape measures, and a much less sophisticated attitude toward his calling.

A lawyer would need a new set of law books, a wig, maybe a gown and certainly a more deferential attitude toward judges.

A reporter can step off a plane in a strange country and go to work. The things he doesn't know about the country are just what his readers will want to know (within limits). If the reporter is writing mainly for American readers, he may turn first to the local American colony to see what it is up to and for general information. But he may discard this approach as chauvinistic and plunge into what may prove to be more interesting paths. This is especially true of interior Africa, parts of which even at this late date are *terra incognita*.

The reporter will find some bizarre developments in black Africa, such as rivalries between Communist and Nationalist

Lynn Heinzerling. The sometime roving AP expert on Africa is shown looking out over the lake created by the great Kariba Dam on the Zambezi River between Zambia and Rhodesia.

Chinese carpetbaggers. The Peking Communists are building a 1,116-mile railroad from the Copper Belt of Zambia to the Indian Ocean port of Dar es Salaam in Tanzania. Elsewhere in Africa both the Communists and Nationalists have applied experts and expertise to increase rice production—with their own motivations; the Communists are obviously trying to spread their national trade and, naturally, their Peking-style revolution. The Nationalists of Taiwan try to retain support of the nations of fragmented Africa that were formerly parts of great empires; those votes are important at the United Nations to keep Taipei as a veto-holding member. And to keep Peking out of the U.N.

Americans and Europeans as well are in the race to fill the vacuum between the twilight of colonialism and the dawn of exotic nationalism amid persisting tribalism.

First and simplest of all, a correspondent can give himself and his readers a geography lesson on the far corner he has chosen to investigate.

The questions the correspondent asks are the questions the reader would ask. And these days you aim at the sophisticated reader.

The big problem for the reporter comes on his third or fourth visit. He already has asked all the obvious questions. He may forget that nobody but God knows everything about a country, a situation, a happening.

What I am saying about a visit to a country is equally true of a baseball game, a court case, or the Beatles. There is always something new to learn, something to invite your curiosity.

And it pays off.

An AP reporter in the Congo once wondered why a certain Belgian colonel hadn't turned up at his usual post as expected early in the morning. He went around to the colonel's billet to inquire about him and found him just leaving for the airport with a platoon of troops.

The AP man was the only newsman present when the Belgians opened fire against the Congolese holding the airport and freed about one hundred hostages.

In Johannesburg one Saturday afternoon in 1960, an AP reporter went to the fairgrounds to hear Prime Minister Hendrik Verwoerd deliver a speech. He heard the speech and phoned the office.

All the other reporters and most of the photographers heard the speech and headed for town. The AP man and an AP photographer waited for Verwoerd to leave. He was still scheduled to present prizes for the best cattle on exhibit.

It was while Verwoerd was performing this humble rite that a man shot him in the head in an attempted assassination. (Verwoerd was assassinated by stabbing six years later).

It doesn't always happen that way. Sometimes, alas, it is the other fellow who shows that last spark of patience and curiosity to get the story.

A Writer Travels Light

There are, of course, some differences between working at home and working abroad. Obstacles crop up on either side of the Atlantic. The most important obstacle over here is language.

It isn't quite true that a good reporter who speaks American can cover anything anywhere. He may eventually catch up with the story, but he will have some unpleasant moments until he gets his lines of communication established. It is handy to have French as a second language and in Africa, of course, Arabic, Swahili and Afrikaans help.

When moving in on a news story, over here or anywhere, it helps to know in advance what you want. You can be working on two or three stories at the same time and ask your questions accordingly. You will obviously get new ideas as you proceed and these are bonuses. They may even provide better stories than those you had in mind.

Knowing what you want, your next step is to consider who is in the best position to supply the information. Every country has an information officer, sometimes dozens of them, excepting, I guess, Ruanda and Burundi (no newspapers there). I seem to be thinking fundamentally of Africa, but the same applies to almost any foreign country.

Some information officers can be helpful; others may be negative if not poisonous. At any rate, it is a good idea to pay your respects, at least on the first visit. But, if you don't want the government to know what you are after, ignore them.

Sometimes it is better to approach the official or the minister you want to see directly through his secretary or assistant. Many dignitaries distrust information officers, considering them meddlers at best.

Embassies are good sources of information, but it is advisable to touch base at two or three of them to get diverse views of political events.

Local businessmen, if the political situation is not too delicate, often will be helpful.

If there is a university in the city, professors are often eager to talk and exhibit their wide knowledge of events.

The editor of the local newspaper is usually delighted to see a foreign newsman and to fill him in, but you must always know his politics. Ministers of the gospel also can be helpful.

Taxi drivers, although much quoted, are about as reliable as the size of your tip.

The first thing to do on entering a strange city is to locate the post office and its cable-receiving counter. If the post office closes at 6 P.M. and you don't know it, you could be dead despite all your news sources.

PETER ARNETT, the only New Zealander ever to win a Pulitzer Prize for war reporting, covered the Vietnam war for eight years for the AP. He won the Pulitzer in 1966, an Overseas Press Club award in 1967, an award of the professional journalistic society Sigma Delta Chi in 1968, and (with AP colleague Horst Faas, a Pulitzer Prize photographer) the 1970 George Polk memorial award of the Overseas Press Club for exceptional courage and enterprise in foreign reporting.

War and Essential Truths

BY PETER ARNETT

Reporting a war is a journalistic gold rush.

The raw copy that makes black headlines is scattered like nuggets across the landscape; the air is heady with the stuff of front pages.

The old Klondike miners looked beyond the nuggets that glinted on the surface. They searched for that source of all wealth, the mother lode.

I see the mother lode as the essential truth that lies somewhere in the mountains of war, chaos and confusion. That is what I tried to mine in Vietnam.

There might be the trace of it on the bomb-blasted aircraft carrier *Forrestal* with its cargo of bodies below decks. Or with the bloodied First Cavalry division at the Ia Drang valley, or at Bo Kinh, a hamlet that uncomplainingly died one day.

And maybe it will appear tantalizingly while I thrash my brain over a news analysis.

The essential truths lie deeper than the surface drama.

I seek this truth in every story I write. It goes beyond fact gathering. It is the development of a central idea that will illuminate an important aspect of the kaleidoscopic war.

On the *Forrestal* it was the sheer horror of how men die, the human torches bobbing and weaving across the deck.

At the Ia Drang it was the brutalizing effect of a war that drove men to kill wounded prisoners.

At Bo Kinh it was the spectacle of civilians sacrificed yet again to achieving a military objective.

And in a news analysis it might be the sudden realization through a maze of statistics, quotes and opinions that things are going either one way or the other, not the time-honored "on the one hand this but on the other hand that."

These essential truths may sometimes be glaringly obvious. Generally, they are hidden below ground and you have to dig deep to find them.

I was attempting to determine the rationale behind the destruction of Ben Tre during the 1968 Tet offensive when a U.S. major did it for me in casual conversation: "We had to destroy the town to save it."

And in trying to illustrate the enthusiasm of the U.S. ninth infantry division in its constant hunt for Vietcong in the northern Mekong Delta I was helped by a U.S. colonel who, after being praised by a senior officer for the large number of kills his helicopter gunships had made the previous week, snapped a salute and commented: "It's our God-given right, sir."

The quotes don't always have to be damning. The war has its noble aspects. But ugliness prevails as much as beauty. The reporter in Vietnam has a major advantage over his colleagues of previous wars: He can tell it as he sees it, the unvarnished truth.

Determining the essential truths is but the beginning. Then comes the writing. I bear in mind the admonition of my college English instructor in New Zealand: "Whatever you write, have consideration for your reader. He has little time. You have to tempt him. Make it worthwhile."

So the idea is more important to me than the adjective. Out with the lyrical turns of phrase, prune down a sentence to its essentials.

Peter Arnett. Correspondent Arnett covers a battle in the bushes of Vietnam.

The complex nature of the Vietnam war almost defies simplification, but you grind on, anyway, whether it is sweating over a typewriter in a press tent at Dak To, or in Saigon waiting for inspiration while the Foreign Desk in New York reminds you of an upcoming deadline.

The deepest truths of the war would be worthless if they were tangled up in verbosity. You have the scaffolding; now to build a tightly organized structure around it. The journalist minor lays down his Geiger counter, picks up a hammer and becomes a journalistic carpenter.

War and Essential Truths

Some reporters may be writing for the Little Old Lady in Dubuque, others for the scholars of the Ivy League. My target is the Portuguese-speaking secretary in Rio de Janeiro, or the Italian farmer.

If I can persuade their favorite newspapers to use my story then I figure I have broken through the communications barrier and done my duty for a worldwide news service.

My proudest compliment came from a translator in the AP Paris bureau who told me they translated my stories direct and unchanged, apparently an infrequent occurrence.

I regard that as a victory with language worth bragging about.

FRANK CORMIER has the last word at presidential news conferences. As the senior news service man at the White House, he ends the questioning of the Chief of State with the traditional, "Thank you, Mr. President." At Dallas, Cormier was in the motorcade when President Kennedy was assassinated and he sped to the local AP office to write developing details as they came in from Parkland hospital and from the oath-taking of the new President Johnson. Prior to becoming head of the AP White House staff in December, 1962, Cormier was the AP's economics expert in Washington, covering the Treasury, the Bureau of the Budget, the Department of Commerce, the Federal Trade Commission, the Federal Reserve and the Securities and Exchange Commission. Cormier has written three books: *Wall Street's Shady Side, Presidents Are People Too,* and (in collaboration with William J. Eaton of the Chicago *Daily News* Washington staff) *Reuther,* a biography of the late Walter Reuther, head of the United Auto Workers.

White House Beat

BY FRANK CORMIER

If you'd enjoy having the President of the United States seek your advice on matters of state, or wouldn't object to being chewed out by him, perhaps you'd like to be a White House reporter. You would not be consulted on policy questions every day, nor would you be chastised on any regular schedule. Sooner or later, however, you would be likely to have both experiences.

The first time I saw John F. Kennedy, he dispensed with small talk and, having been briefed on my earlier work as an Associated Press economics reporter, he asked what I would do to solve the balance-of-payments problem. I told him but he dismissed my ideas remarking, "We can handle that by jiggering interest rates."

The last time we talked together, four days before he was assassinated in Dallas, Kennedy rebuked me for what he considered unwarranted prying into his personal affairs. Quite by chance, our paths had crossed in a hotel lobby after midnight and he mistakenly decided I had been waiting there to determine the hour of his return from a private party.

From the viewpoint of White House newsmen, Kennedy was a recluse compared with Lyndon B. Johnson, whose contacts with the press were much more frequent and far more intimate.

On a flight around the world in 1967, Johnson asked six of us who were aboard Air Force One, the presidential plane, whether he should go to Rome and see Pope Paul VI. Promising to abide by our decision, the President offered the alternative of a visit to Madrid. Knowing we were weary from our journey, Johnson announced we could get a night's rest in a hotel in Madrid, but if we chose Rome the stop there would be brief and would be followed immediately by an overnight flight back to Washington. Our reply was unanimous: the decision could be made only by the President, based on his own assessment of his duty and the requirements of the national interest. He saw the Pope.

Circling the earth is a thrilling experience under almost any circumstance. Yet the Johnson trip, despite its full ration of excitement, was extremely demanding of both the President and the press. Together we circumnavigated the planet in just four and a half days—and spent only one night in a hotel. Two members of the press corps collapsed along the way and were left behind in hospitals, one in Australia and the other in a remote part of Thailand.

Soundness of wind and limb is a requisite for White House reporters. Consider some of the repeated tests of stamina: Running for helicopters, motorcades and telephones. Pitting your strength against crowds pressing in from all sides. Taking off on short notice, sometimes without baggage, for distant places. And, in spurts that seem to pile up in clumps, working for abnormal periods of time while trying to shake off numbing fatigue and retain an ability to dictate major, fast-breaking news developments instantly and off the cuff.

When President Nixon circled the globe in 1969, we reporters who accompanied him lived through three working days that approached, and even exceeded, twenty-four hours from wake up to lie down. One of these was climaxed by a policy-stating news conference on Guam—the first enunciation of the Nixon Doctrine—and another by a memorable welcome in Communist Romania. If one was to single out a day of extreme excitement and fatigue, it would be the one that for many reporters began

Frank Cormier. He leads a strenuous and exacting life watching the President as best he can at the White House, in the air and on the road. Here is Cormier (second from right, in picture above) with former President Johnson and other newsmen at Stonewall, Texas, and at a news conference (at left, in picture below) questioning President Nixon.

before dawn aboard the carrier *Hornet,* where we witnessed the recovery of the first men to set foot on the moon, continued with the Guam news conference, and ended many hours later in Manila.

With the excitements of that trip in mind, newsmen later comparing notes on their most arduous days on the job almost forgot one that began on Guam with a Vietnam summit meeting, in 1967, and ended with a flight back to Washington on which we witnessed two sunsets.

Even Hyannis Port, Key Biscayne and San Clemente, for all their attractions, can with the passage of time have their drawbacks. For one thing, we have to leave our wives and children home. Most of us, at least initially, found Lyndon Johnson's native hill country of central Texas beautiful, even fascinating. After making several dozen trips there a month at a time, however, feeding on a sparse diet of news while the President recuperated from surgery became a mind-dulling experience. One reporter found his own prescription for fighting boredom: "Let's go out and watch a few haircuts."

The occasional glamour that goes with the job of being a White House newsman must be balanced against the hard work, the many drab days when you feel like a fireman waiting for the alarm that never sounds—and reprimands you're likely to get, if you stick around long enough, from the President himself.

Johnson once invaded a briefing session by his secretary of agriculture, Orville Freeman, to lecture me in front of my colleagues about an article I'd written—an accurate article, I insist. On another occasion, he lit into me—for a question I'd asked at a news conference—at an intimate luncheon in the family dining room at the White House; perhaps he hoped I'd be fired, since the few people present included the AP general manager, Wes Gallagher, and the AP Washington bureau chief, Marvin Arrowsmith, himself a former White House correspondent.

These Johnsonian incidents, and others of the same vein, had counterbalances. One could not forget, for example, that Lyndon Johnson was more accessible to the press than, almost certainly, any other President. And there were the many kindnesses, small and large, that he showed us. We had to accept his mood of the moment, and often we enjoyed it.

In short, White House reporters have an exposure to Presidents unequaled among others outside government, save for the relatives and personal friends of the chief executive. We will not forget, for instance, the Christmas parties for us at the Kennedy house in Palm Beach, with the eye-popping toys of Caroline and young John still under the tree; the tours of the LBJ Ranch personally conducted by the President himself followed by the serving of Texas-size hamburger steaks in the ranch dining room; lunching with President Nixon in a Mexican-American restaurant at San Juan Capistrano, and Pat Nixon kneeling in the aisle of Air Force One, passing out candy and chitchat.

Although Presidents spend much time away from Washington, with the press going along only because whatever the top man does or says is of interest to someone—as when a single county in one state is declared a Federal disaster area, eligible for special Federal financial assistance – most days find White House reporters at the White House.

Our pattern there, with periodic and noteworthy exceptions, follows a predictable routine. Until early 1970, we gathered each morning in the reception lobby of the West Wing of the White House, a few yards from the President's oval office. If there were telephone calls to make, or there was work to do, we stepped a few feet into what had served for decades as the White House press room—cramped quarters just off the lobby where there were no secrets. Any lounger could overhear the business of anyone ten feet away—and that included most of us.

Pressed for office space for key assistants, notably foreign policy adviser Henry A. Kissinger, consigned at the time to the White House basement, Nixon began thinking of alternatives that would free our space for staff use. First he considered digging out a small part of the front lawn and burying us there. We objected, and the people assigned to restrain Federal spending objected more strongly. The underground press room was forgotten.

Nixon, however, had his way in rescuing Kissinger from the

basement. Now we inhabit quarters over the preserved but hidden swimming pool built for Franklin D. Roosevelt. We have a lounge-briefing room, two press rooms, two additional lounges and a vending machine canteen. Such luxury we had never known. The main lounge is decorated by the folks from colonial Williamsburg, who even selected the prints on the wall. A colleague taking his first view remarked, "If you don't mind, I'll stay and have a drink but I won't go upstairs with the girls."

We congregate in these relatively plush quarters about 9 A.M., which normally is an hour or two in advance of the first announced presidential appointment of the day. The length of our daily stay in Babylon-cum-Williamsburg is dictated by the President's schedule and—most important—by an announcement from the press office that there is a "Lid"—an end to public, reportable activity. The Lid can come as early as 4:30 P.M. or it may, at a time of crisis, extend into the following day.

Between starting time and The Lid, however, reporters and photographers are invited, at the President's pleasure, to witness and record some segments of his daily routine. He calls the shots. If it's a public appearance, everyone normally is granted "full coverage"—reporting, filming, recording. Even then, as we have learned, a President may demand that only one side of his face be photographed; the one I'm thinking of happened to believe he had only one good profile. If it's a formal speech, cameramen may be shooed away after a few minutes—depending on who's boss—lest a candid shot prove to be an embarrassment. On those occasions, more frequent in the Johnson years than with Nixon, television and newsreel cameras are allowed to keep grinding away after the still photographers—those who take pictures for newspapers and magazines—are banished. This kind of discrimination-by-media has never contributed to harmony.

If a President is meeting someone in his oval office, or in the neighboring Rose Garden, reporters and photographers may or may not be invited to watch and record what is to be seen and heard. Some of the most newsworthy sessions go unrecorded. When Nixon held a Vietnam policy conference with key advisors in September, 1969, for example, the press office declared beforehand that no photographs would be permitted. At the last minute, however, a few cameramen and reporters were let in—for forty seconds only. Despite the enormous attention attracted by the meeting, no participant talked to any reporter at the White House. Those cornered elsewhere and later were uncommunicative.

Because the White House staff is relatively small, although ever growing, and is under direct presidential command, reporters often find that trying to pry information out of assistants to a chief executive is more frustrating than enlightening. If ever there was an exception to the general rule, it was during the Kennedy administration. Jack Kennedy surrounded himself with talkative, bright and, in some instances, attention-seeking aides. Newsmen occasionally found themselves in the unaccustomed position then of trying to get a presidential aide to quit talking so they could go about their business.

This never proved to be a hallmark of the Johnson or Nixon administrations. Dr. Kissinger, as Nixon's national security assistant, never cottoned to the notion of having his staff talk to the press—despite the fact that the pressures of his job, as his apologists were quick to explain, would not permit him to act as press spokesman in any adequate fashion. Yet his predecessors, McGeorge Bundy and Walt Whitman Rostow, knew and talked to a far broader range of reporters. Kissinger, however, once willing to step forward, often seems more forthright, less patronizing and perhaps more candid, than those who preceded him in the job.

Because the White House is a tight little island, many major news breaks in any administration come from knowledgeable people in Federal agencies or on Capitol Hill. Newsmen often discover that helpfulness from these sources depends on degree of distance, geographically, personally or ideologically, from the White House.

Of course, presidential press secretaries do talk. At least, words come out of their mouths, normally twice a day, Monday through Friday, at morning and afternoon briefings for White House reporters and any other accredited correspondents who care to drop by. Mimeographed press releases are supplemented by oral announcements and it sometimes is possible to get a direct answer to a direct question. Many inquiries, however, receive no meaningful replies because the subjects involved concern matters the President or his press secretary do not want to discuss.

As in any police department press room, frustration and boredom alternate with challenge and excitement at 1600 Pennsylvania Avenue. It should be noted, though, that there are differences. The White House press room has a carpet on the floor.

The AP Science Editor, ALTON BLAKESLEE, a prolific writer himself, directs a staff of specialists covering subjects ranging from the earth's ecology to man's footprints on the moon. His numerous prizes in more than a quarter-century of science writing include two American Heart Association awards named for his late father, Howard W. Blakeslee, a pioneer AP science writer-editor. Alton Blakeslee's daughter Sandra, a third generation science writer, is with *The New York Times*.

Science Writing: An Art of Translation

BY ALTON BLAKESLEE

In reporting science, there is no such thing as a dumb question.

The injunction applies, of course, to all stories, but perhaps particularly to science and medicine because the specialists talk with one another in technical language. It is their shorthand; it is effective, if sometimes indulged as a mark of snobbishness.

The science writer is in part a translator from the arcane language of science. He needs only to remind himself that not everyone speaks chemistry or physics or medicine, or Hindustani. His readers do speak and read English. They are receptive to the ideas and concepts and contributions from science and medicine, when the writing is in their own tongue. They are usually interested, or can be enticed into interest, in affairs that affect their lives significantly.

A concept I find useful is to regard readers as people who are not ignorant but who may be *innocent* of the fields I am reporting. They are intelligent, and they have intelligent questions about the story I write.

Therefore, it is not a dumb question when you ask that a technical word be defined in simple terms, when you probe for an understanding of a complex concept, when you ask whether a

Science Writing: An Art of Translation

medication has real or potential harmful or bothersome side effects as well as benefit and value.

Good scientists and good doctors do not mind the dumb question if you make it clear you want answers in order to be totally accurate. Good scientists and physicians—as much as they might prefer your having some background about their subjects, or your having taken some pains to learn the rudiments of their field if you had had the time—are eager to inform a serious listener. They like and are enthusiastic about what they are doing in life, and they want to share that interest and enthusiasm.

In interviews, never feel intimidated by the specialists and their specialized bits of lore. All are human beings. You are also performing a specialized job—writing for the general public, in language as simple, as clear and as interesting as you can possibly make it. The astronomer can puzzle a chemist by speaking only in his own jargon, and vice versa. And the housewife with her technical terms in cooking could puzzle them both.

The science or medical story requires your learning far more than you will be able to write within space limitations, or even within interest limitations. You need to understand the subject, as fully as possible, in order to write about it briefly. Only by knowing the relative importance of details, and the relationships of concepts can you do the shorthand of writing concisely, and still remain accurate.

Writing reflects the writer. If he is not interested in his subject it surely shows. So push your enthusiasm button with each story —it is either really worth writing or else junk it.

Digest your information, then tell it. Sometimes it helps to tell it orally to someone else. This distills your own thinking, and the hard part of writing is not pushing the typewriter keys but doing the thinking. Irreverence may even help. One sport among science writers—and other specialists or generalists as well—is to make up leads you cannot use. A medical research report once told of finding a higher incidence of cancer of the uterus among virgins than among married women. The unused lead was, "Cancer is a form of rust, not lust." But it helped put the story on the way.

Alton Blakeslee. As the AP Science Editor he has the job of simplifying without oversimplifying the scientific milieu, from the lab and test tube to man's conquests in Outer Space.

Inevitably the science–medical story must, even should, use some technical terms, because they are so accurate. Use the word —but define it immediately, at that spot, or in the next sentence. Then you can use it again—in that story only, until a word like "orbit" becomes part of the general language.

Use similes—compare the unfamiliar with the familiar, to depict meaning and significance—use description. Earth's gravity pull, which astronauts must escape to go to the moon, can be compared with a car coasting up hill. It will crest the hill if it has enough initial speed. Frequently, your source, the specialist, will

Science Writing: An Art of Translation 97

volunteer a beautiful simile or metaphor. He has usually thought of the problem of explaining his work clearly; he may have tried to explain it to his children, wife, or neighbors who were innocents about his work.

By the bye, before becoming critical of a specialist's work, before putting the hard questions if you think you have them, first draw him out. Let him speak; encourage the talk and explanations. Then begin putting questions as a nonspecialist to whom the work or experiment seems to have holes.

Then comes the writing. Find and express the most interesting aspects in a short news story. In a longer feature story find the human qualities and establish a pace.

Be dissatisfied until you have found a good lead. The lead, in a science story, will also dictate construction in part. One idea must logically lead to another, or to an explanation of what was said in the preceding paragraph. Beware of the quicksand of too many details, however appealing they may be to you, unless you have space and can be clear and interesting in the excursions into details. Spare the adjectives except for the most stunning events.

Over the years, I remember only one really easy lead. At the end of a Christmas-holiday science meeting in Berkeley, California, officials announced the winner of a $1,000 prize given annually to a young scientist, under thirty-five, who had presented the best paper. That year, it went to a Pittsburgh scientist who had created the nearest to a perfect vacuum yet produced in the laboratory. The scientist explained to a news conference how he had done it. He compared it with the presumed vacuum in space. The hour was 5 P.M., in California—meaning 8 P.M. in Pittsburgh, which would be most keen for the story.

Fortunately, the lead sprang to mind and the story was all done in five minutes. The lead: "A young scientist today won $1,000 for making the most of nothing."

HOWARD BENEDICT, the first designated AP aerospace writer, has covered more than 1,800 rocket launchings, including all the U.S. man-in-space shots and the landings on the moon. The job was undreamed of when he began newspapering at age fifteen in Sioux City, Iowa. His professional prizes make a long list.

Space: Up from Bird Watch Hill

BY HOWARD BENEDICT

Secrecy was the name of the game when I was assigned in 1959 to cover the missile beat at what was then Cape Canaveral and now is Cape Kennedy.

Those were the days of the missile gap and rockets with names like Thor, Jupiter, Snark, Bold Orion, Matador, Hound Dog and Green Quail. There were more failures than successes, and an exploding Atlas or Polaris was a common sight.

So many Snarks plunged into the Atlantic after takeoff that newsmen decided the waters off Cape Canaveral were Snark-infested.

The Polaris was an Intermediate Range Ballistic Missile, or IRBM. When one of these stubby submarine rockets went wild, skimmed over a trailer court and plunged into the Banana River west of the Cape, reporters dubbed it an IBRM—In the Banana River Missile.

Congressmen were asking why all the failures. The Air Force clamped a secrecy lid on missile operations, including launching dates.

Newsmen usually had an inkling when a missile was to be launched, and often camped on a high sandy knoll on the beach

—which we nicknamed Bird Watch Hill—with cameras aimed at the launching pads.

The Air Force knew it couldn't hide a missile once it was launched. They made too much noise, especially when they blew up. But defense officials said the shape of a missile was classified, and they objected to our taking pictures.

Very often, just before a rocket took off, an Air Force helicopter would zoom in on Bird Watch Hill, hovering to stir up sand and scatter the newsmen. By the time the cameramen reassembled, the rocket was out of sight. No pictures.

We gradually became smarter and more sophisticated. We developed sources in many of the programs and often learned when a missile was to be launched and its general test purpose.

A big break came when I learned through amateur radio friends that we could monitor countdowns if we had the proper equipment. The count had to be transmitted to down-range stations so they could be ready—and Russian trawlers stood off shore to intercept the signals.

If the Russians could do it, why couldn't we? So the AP invested in radio-receiving equipment for our beachside office, whose balcony also had a high-power telescope to keep track of activity on Cape Canaveral.

The radio worked. Countdowns came through loud and clear. No longer did we have to waste hours watching the Cape. The radio also provided information, such as whether a missile succeeded or failed as it streaked down range.

There were visits from representatives of the Federal Bureau of Investigation, the office of Special Investigations, and the Office of Naval Intelligence. All asked the same question: Where are you getting your information?

They finally figured out the radio—since it was sitting in plain view every time they visited the office. The range tried scrambling the countdown signals. But a couple of times a tracking station had difficulty decoding them quickly, and by the time it did the missile had passed it by. Scrambling was abandoned.

All the while, members of the press corps met frequently with Air Force officials and bombarded the Defense Department with

Space: Up from Bird Watch Hill

letters and phone calls, asking for a more liberal policy on the release of news on launchings.

The fact that we were obtaining so much information independently helped the cause. Then, about six months after my arrival, the Atlas and Polaris—the big stick rockets—began working. The Defense Department felt more inclined to discuss results—to get Congress off its back.

An agreement was reached. Newsmen would be briefed each Friday on the launch schedule for the following week and would be given general information on the purpose of the tests. We would be taken to a press site at the Cape for each launch.

We agreed not to write about a launching in advance. The rule: Report when there's fire in the tail.

Since then the rule has been relaxed considerably, and we have been permitted to announce many military firings five days before a launch date.

The space age was in its infancy when I arrived at Cape Canaveral. The National Aeronautics and Space Administration (NASA) was only seven months old and had launched only a few satellites.

Newsmen were permitted to cover the launchings from the Cape press site. But the Air Force fire-in-the-tail directive applied and we could not report the shot in advance.

We had many conferences with NASA officials. Our main argument: There is a big difference between a scientific space shot and a military test firing. The public is entitled to know as much as possible about a scientific project for which it is paying a lot of money.

We persevered and prevailed. We were permitted to announce a satellite shot a day in advance, then five days, then thirty days—and today there is no limit. As soon as NASA sets a launch schedule, it becomes public knowledge.

There were many problems when man started flying into space. When astronaut Alan Shepard made America's first flight, NASA's policy was to release his name after the rocket left the Cape.

Officials kept his identity a closely guarded secret. But the AP

Howard Benedict. The AP's No. 1 aerospace writer (left) with astronaut Wally Schirra and an AP colleague, Paul Recer (right).

learned it was Shepard a few hours before the launch and reported it urgently.

There was a gradual transformation on the name-the-astronaut policy.

On the second flight, NASA announced Virgil Grissom's name one day before the launch, although we, again through sources, had it two weeks before.

Space: Up from Bird Watch Hill

John Glenn's name was announced two weeks before his scheduled flight. Now the astronaut crews are unveiled months in advance.

As the space age evolved, space reporters have had to learn the terminology and views of scientists, astronomers, technicians and engineers in order to understand the intricacies of the job and to report them in understandable language to the nation's readers and listeners.

This has required hours of meetings with experts, most of whom have been very patient and willing to teach.

As each launching becomes more complex than the last, we must do our homework. We have to comprehend the nuts and bolts of the remarkable things we're writing about.

The emphasis is on manned space flight. During the Mercury program we had to explain how rockets work, what an orbit is, how a spacecraft stays up, how the astronaut stays alive, what re-entry is.

In the Gemini program, we described how a spaceship is maneuvered, how astronauts rendezvous and dock with another satellite, how they survive while walking in space.

At the end of the Gemini program in late 1966, NASA was ready to move directly into Apollo, and a moon landing seemed possible by as early as 1968. But then tragedy struck the program when astronauts Virgil I. Grissom, Edward H. White II and Roger Chaffee died in a spaceship cabin fire during a routine launch-pad test in January, 1967.

Attention turned to the long investigation and the hearings in Congress, with the resulting condemnation of the space agency and its main spaceship contractor, North American Aviation, for negligence, poor workmanship and improper management.

I spent considerable time in Washington on the hearings and probing into the background for investigative stories. With the investigation over, reporting concentrated on the long road back —the overhaul in management and machinery that led to resumption of manned flights with Apollo 7 in October, 1968.

Then followed the nine most interesting and exciting months

a reporter could experience. In that time there were five almost flawless Apollo missions, culminating in the historic moon landing and the momentous moon walk by astronauts Neil A. Armstrong and Edwin E. Aldrin Jr. on July 20, 1969.

There were some unforgettable moments in that stretch—the Apollo 8 moon orbit, the testing of the lunar lander in earth orbit on Apollo 9, Apollo 10's descent to within nine miles of the moon's surface and Armstrong's memorable: "That's one small step for a man; one giant leap for mankind."

Because of the immense interest, Apollo 11 required thousands of words of explanation—everything from how a spaceship escapes earth's gravity to how the lunar vehicle lands on the moon.

More than 3,000 newsmen descended on Cape Kennedy for the Apollo 11 launching.

Most had a hard time believing the tales of the early days at Cape Canaveral.

For they were inundated with masses of background material on the mission. There were press kits by the score from NASA and the industrial contractors.

There were daily background briefings on all aspects of the flight. Throughout the flight—when we shifted from the Cape to the Manned Spacecraft Center in Houston—the astronauts' voices were piped live into news communications channels. For a few dollars, a reporter could have the telephone company install a circuit that funneled the entire mission commentary into his motel room.

Personally, I prepared for months for Apollo 11. Because in the long run it's the individual interviews that provide the most information. The long talks with the flight controllers, the rocket experts, the policy makers and the astronauts themselves.

Three weeks before each manned launching, including Apollo 11, the three major radio-TV networks and the news services are permitted private interviews with each of the astronauts who make the flight. These tape-recorded sessions, plus personal contacts with the spacemen, are most valuable for injecting a pilot's deep feelings into the reporting of a flight.

We've come a long way from the days of Bird Watch Hill.

JOHN BARBOUR has reported the space program from the outset as a science news and feature writer and specializes now as well on environment and conservation. He is author of the AP space book, *Footprints on the Moon,* and co-author of others; he wrote a paperback on allergy and a book on the near extinction of the blue whale, *In the Wake of the Whale.*

Science, Environment & Conservation

BY JOHN BARBOUR

Writing about environment you can start anywhere.

Too often we tend to look at environment as water and air. And we tend to think of it as something new—dirty old mankind contaminating his world with smoke and sewage. That definition is too narrow. And the subject is not new. It's as old as dirty old mankind itself.

Environment is the world we live in, all of that world. The problems of environment come from too many of us, living too close together and demanding too much of our world.

The reporter or writer or editor ought to consider something more than smog and polluted streams. He ought to consider all of those forces that alter people's lives in ways that are dangerous or just uncomfortable. A story on the high smog level of Tuesday, February 11, in Anytown or the sewage dumped by the paper mill upstream, or the fish kill caused by rising temperatures in the waters ought to provide more than the small facts. It ought to consider the larger facts, the dynamics that brought it all about. The increase in population that brought on the increase in cars, why the paper mill located where it did and how long ago and is it worse now or has it always been this way.

Science, Environment & Conservation 107

Furthermore the reporter should seek out people who do more than measure and chronicle the problems. He should seek out the people with ideas of how to solve them.

Webster defines environment as "the surrounding conditions, influences, or forces, which influence or modify."

The loss of vacant lots is an environmental problem. So are the noises from the upstairs apartment, the drunk on the train, the narcotics peddler at the high school, the packaging of meats at the supermarket.

A young architect says, "I'm not going to build houses for people to live in until I learn more about how people live and how people want to live." You mean life is more than bedroom, bathroom and kitchen?

In most communities you can't burn leaves any more, but in the old days the smoke of burning leaves used to flavor the autumn air. We live too close together to allow old extravagances. There are too many of us. Urban crowding has become suburban crowding, and people are problems of the environment. So then birth control is a problem of environment, and the way birth control affects the mores of people is a problem of environment.

Almost all the things that affect the quality of life are problems of environment.

The person who covers that kind of story has to know something about how people live and how they want to live. He has to know something of history and something of the law. But the problems have accumulated so fast that few people except the conservationists have gathered that kind of information.

Almost all of the natural resources taken from the earth have been dug and drilled and pumped up since 1910, barely sixty years ago. Great gaping pits scar the earth, mountains are missing, the iron ore is turned into steel to be turned into cars to be turned into rusting piles of junk, and the coal and oil carted to the cities are converted into brown and black gaseous sludge in the air.

Consider the whales. The Blue Whale was the largest creature that ever lived, as large as thirty elephants or three of the biggest

John Barbour. He is a member of the AP team writing on exploits in space, author of the book Footprints on the Moon *and several works on environment and conservation, and a general reporter on science subjects. Above, he writes the morning paper leads on the Apollo 11 moonshot.*

dinosaurs. Yet the Blue Whale is nearly extinct. It was hauled from the sea to provide everything from oil for street lamps to fertilizer for fields. It took nature 100 million years to create the whale, and man only fifty years to destroy it.

Conservationists, worried about the whale, suggest we ought to be concerned about the law as it governs the sea in general. The legal idea of the early seas was *res nullius,* which meant essentially that the seas belonged to no one. No one could say stop. No one could exert control. More practically, suggest the conservationists,

Science, Environment & Conservation 109

the time has come to look at the seas as *res communis,* as belonging to everyone. Then no one could pillage the seas or the things that live there without stealing from the common welfare.

The same principle is being applied to the air, rivers, schools, apartment building and potentially everything else in our way of life. In a city like New York people are asking whether the landlord who doesn't care has as much to say about his building as the people who live in it.

Who are the sources for a story on the environment, and on conservation of the environment? Certainly more than the people who sound the alarm, and even more than the people affected. Certainly more than the politicians who echo the public displeasure.

Local lawyers or the nearest law school can offer a good picture of the legalities involved. The nearby college can provide the engineering and scientific background on how other areas dealt with similiar problems. Sometimes a social scientist can tell your readers the dynamics that set the problem up.

People get pecked to death by smog statistics. They know there is smog. They want to know why, and where it comes from and why something isn't being done about it. Send a reporter wandering through the basements with the local furnace inspectors. Send someone over to do a story on the municipal incinerator. Talk to the man who runs it, and get a garbage man's view of the changing seasons. Ask him what it looks like after Halloween.

The bumper-to-bumper motorist, the housewife trying to see the underside of a chuck roast in a sealed package, the garbage man toting away the things that won't burn and won't decay, they all know problems of their environments. They are all good story sources.

Environment is the nonreturnable bottle, the nondegradable detergent, the constant stream of conveniences that are foisted on people who are never asked whether they want them. If these products are for sale, they are bought, not because of their packaging but because of what is in them. Conveniences? For whom? The manufacturer or the consumer?

If newspapers are the link between people and the structure of their community, they can also be the link between the consumer and the manufacturer. But what story on environmental problems in a city tracks down the heap of glass that emerges from the fires of the municipal incinerator and then goes to the people of the town and asks them if they really want nonreturnable bottles? Are those bottles a convenience? Tally up the amount of tax money spent on finding and leasing new areas for sanitary fill, places to dispose of the nondisposable. Get someone to estimate the increased garbage load in the last ten years due solely to packages that can't be destroyed. Did it cost the city a dozen new trucks? Wouldn't it be awful if the nonreturnable bottle cost every taxpayer in town something like 3 dollars a year or maybe thirty dollars a year? Is it worth it? Only the reader can answer that one.

Pollution problems can't be covered in depth from the state house, in legislative hearings. In a sense the legislators are the last to know. People feel so frustrated by the enormity of government and the merchandising structure of our society that many newspapers have in recent years instituted action columns to give their problems a voice. Their questions in these columns are often pleas. And they speak for the way people feel about their environment.

Those columns have the germs of many stories on the environment. They also communicate the idea that the world is falling apart. For the average American the environment is the quality of his life, and it has to be covered that way.

ROBERT BERRELLEZ for years had the longest news beat in the world—from the Mexican border (where he was born at Nogales, Arizona) to the tip of South America. Until his early retirement, he was the AP roving correspondent for Latin America. He was jailed under two Latin dictatorships, in Venezuela and Castro's Cuba. In 1968 he won the Maria Moors Cabot award (gold medal and $1,000) for excellence in Latin American news coverage.

The Latin American Beat

BY ROBERT BERRELLEZ

By asking a roomful of reporters for directions to the men's room, Dick Duncan of *Time* magazine once inadvertently touched off a scene of uproarious misunderstanding and confusion. It happened on a story of pre-election rioting in Panama.

Most reporters had crowded into the downtown cable office to send their stories on a messy cleanup of an antigovernment demonstration by National Guardsmen using rifle butts and tear gas. Duncan had stayed behind to pick up additional details and only his natural need took him off course.

In the air-conditioned cable office, Duncan, lapsing into the vernacular of his navy officer days, asked of no one in particular: "Where's the head?"

"Head" unfortunately sounds like "lead" and "dead," and so the panic was on to find the "lead" (bullets) and the "dead."

This is an example of how wild rumors—and wilder stories—often are born in Latin America. If it's true that rumor is the child of poor communication, rich imagination and loose tongues, then this explains why rumor is so abundant in a world of scarcities. Its pervasive presence in the daily routine of life south of the Rio Grande makes news reporting in Latin America perhaps a trifle hazardous and certainly enjoyable.

This is not to say one requires great special skills to do an adequate reporting job. I would rate patience along with language as the prime requisites. These plus a sense of humor, some inventiveness, and small supplies of detergent will see one through most situations.

A crash course in Spanish will provide an excellent base from which to start learning the Latin American varieties of the language. There are some startling differences in the Spanish spoken by Latin Americans. They can mousetrap the unwary into indelicate situations. For instance, one way of asking a lady friend in Caracas to have a drink can mean, in Mexico, an invitation to share a bed. A seemingly innocuous conversational offering about your target practice can be interpreted in some countries as a report that you're taking sex lessons.

I grew up in a Spanish-speaking home in Arizona and it was a shock to learn subsequently in Colombia—my first Latin American assignment twenty years ago—that my Spanish there was less than insufficient. Ten years later, it took months of daily listening to four- and five-hour Fidel Castro harangues to feel adequately geared to the Cuban dictator's Caribbean brand of Spanish.

One of Castro's favorite sports was to keep newsmen waiting three, four and five or more hours for an audience. Not infrequently, reporters discovered they'd been waiting for a man who wasn't in town. One enterprising reporter cast aside scruples and talked a bilingual girl friend into calling Castro's office to determine whether he was in town. The girl was told to tell Castro's secretary this was a call from President Eisenhower's White House office in Washington; if Castro came to the phone the girl was to hang up. The secretary told the caller Castro was out but would be available in an hour and, surprisingly, asked if the call had anything to do with a visit to Washington. This was the first public knowledge of Castro's plans to visit Washington in April 1959.

Waiting for the laundry could be as frustrating as waiting for Castro. And like Castro, the laundry might never show up. So, a few helpful hints from the experienced traveler for those who will have to travel light: 1. Latin American supermarkets carry detergent in small plastic pouches. 2. A pair of scissors applied to a pillowcase can produce useful boxer-type shorts which can be held up with a long piece of material scissored from the same pillow case. The transaction shows on the hotel bill as "miscellany" and on the expense account as perhaps "postage."

The vagaries of laundry provided an interesting sidelight to the story of a 1963 uprising in Honduras. After the government was overthrown by the military, wild shooting broke out in the heart of Tegucigalpa. Most of the North American news crowd was pinned down in the Hotel Prado lobby where the cable and telephone office was fortunately located.

The shooting ignited a fuel tank on the hotel roof and the top floor was burning. Recalling that our make-do laundry was drying on the roof, some of us raced upstairs in hopes of rescuing it. The shooting sounded louder and we got the impression that a lot of the firing was coming from the tops of buildings. A chambermaid came to the rescue. Saying *"un minuto,"* she got a large bedsheet and waved it at the rooftop level. The shooting in our immediate area died down. The fire was not as bad as we had imagined and most of our clothes were salvaged, though singed. But what caught our attention was the number of soldiers squatting on our and nearby rooftops seemingly unconcerned with the sniping. They sat there and looked at us while in the distance we could see other troops firing at nothing in particular.

The maid explained that the soldiers had been up on the roof since early morning and had told her not to worry if she heard shooting because they were just practicing. A few quick questions to some of the soldiers confirmed the maid's story. Questions in the right places later disclosed that troops had been posted on rooftops with orders to begin shooting at a certain hour, at targets like blank walls, advertising signs and at the clouds overhead. The reason?

To those of us familiar with the thinking that sometimes goes into Latin American coups it was an old trick. The idea, we gathered, was to create the illusion, mostly among the foreign press, of a countercoup effort by Marxist revolutionaries against

Robert Berrellez. Ebullient and resourceful were the words to portray him as he made the rounds of Latin America for years. With cap and pipe, he rides behind the then newly elected President of Panama, Dr. Arnulfo Arias, down the Chucunaque River, in a twenty-five foot boat that was a hollowed-out tree trunk driven by outboard motor. As they approached a nearby village, nine shots were fired, splashing in the water near the boat and wounding one passenger.

the new regime. This would justify the claims of the new overlord that he had acted to "preserve democracy" by overthrowing a constitutionally elected government that had been "dangerously infiltrated by extremists."

The rooftop fire ate through the cable company's transmitting equipment and the real story of the latest Honduran blowup did not get out until the following day.

One of the more trying experiences in covering Latin America is avoiding emotional involvement in a world of suffocating poverty, cruelty and corruption and an aching disparity in standards of living. The temptation to champion the little guy against the big one is almost irresistible. This may explain the presence of a new breed of cat among correspondents covering Latin America—the journalist who is more a participant or activist than disinterested observer. A minuscule minority among correspondents, he is the fellow who has brought with him some inflexible concepts and prejudices, the one who spends most of his time talking to one particular segment of the population and whose questions at news conferences soon develop a recognizable slant.

He is part of the challenge in covering this sometimes difficult area. It's no trade secret that some of these reporter-crusaders have tried—in subtle and other ways—to win over news agency reporters to a particular point of view in order to reinforce their own. Some results have been funny.

Following the 1963 military coup that ousted President Juan Bosch from power in the Dominican Republic, one correspondent approached me in the lobby of the Hotel Embajador and announced he had just completed a survey for his paper showing that ninety per cent of the Dominican people opposed the overthrow of Bosch. Just to test the brainwash line, I replied that coincidentally I had just finished a similar survey showing exactly the opposite.

The anticipated reaction led to a friendly wager: We would jointly conduct a quickie survey among hotel employees to see who was right. I felt on safe grounds, having explored coup sentiment several days previously among the hotel workers. It was agreed we would begin with the elevator operator, who said the coup was long overdue. The infuriated correspondent turned on the operator with, "What kind of a Dominican are you?" And that killed the survey idea.

But the crusader can be helpful. Every viewpoint helps shape a larger, multifaceted image of a situation that's to be explored. One correspondent complained to other reporters he had been ousted from the rebel sector of Santo Domingo and that this represented a violation of press freedom the rebels had pledged to uphold. A check turned up something interesting: The correspondent had indeed been asked to leave, but in order to save his life. A group of extreme leftists had been seen with the correspondent, whom the rebels recognized as an ideological adversary. They threatened to kill him. Moving to avoid a serious problem, the rebel official asked the correspondent to leave. This was the first indication that these extremists had come into the open in what turned out to be a determined effort to block peace negotiations in the Dominican civil war.

Excepting the rural areas, food in most Latin American countries is generally on a level with that available in the United States. A popular misconception among North Americans is that Latin American food requires an asbestos-lined stomach. Mexico and a few Central American countries do thrive on hot chile. In most places, you have to ask even for ordinary pepper. Away from the beaten paths, however, you're likely to be confronted with some unusual items like snake, house cat and lizard. The delicious red berry-like nuts we ate by the bagful while covering the visit of Pope Paul VI to Colombia turned out to be big jungle ants, roasted. The best thing to do in the rural areas is not to be too inquisitive over what's on the plate before you. It isn't polite, for one thing, and, most important, there may be nothing else. Whatever it is you've eaten you can always wash down with local firewater—except that a bit too much of the latter invariably makes you hungry for whatever it was that made you turn to the booze before.

And aside from a strong stomach, you'll need a strong bottom to cover some rural areas via mule, donkey, carts and canoes.

What you don't need strong is will. Never make up your mind not to do something. By turning down an invitation to a canoe ride in order to clean up an expense account, one correspondent missed the scene when riverside snipers shot at Panama's President Arnulfo Arias, who had invited the press corps on the trip.

There are exceptions that can result in embarrassment and nasty notes from the boss. But after twenty years it all seems like a ball.

Jules Loh

JULES LOH has roamed the United States from the oil strike in Alaska to the misdoings of Billy Sol Estes in Texas, from George Wallace on the stump to race riots almost everywhere. He is a master of word portraiture, numbering such people as Herbert Hoover, Alfred M. Landon and artist Thomas Hart Benton among those he profiled. He has collaborated on several AP books as well as two of the news service's longest stories, *The Middle Aged Lions* (with Saul Pett) and *The USS Pueblo—The Ship that Went Out in the Cold,* an account of the spy ship affair in North Korea.

Features Without Rhinestones, Please

BY JULES LOH

A dozen years of feature writing lead to three basic observations. Discovering them earlier might have spared me a good deal of agony. Not that writing becomes easier after long practice—new agonies spring up to replace the old as surely as mushrooms after rain. But I might at least have gotten to the new ones sooner.

Observation One is that some writers, and some editors, have a notion that the feature writer's art involves decorating what essentially is a news story with clusters of literary rhinestones. It doesn't. A good feature story is unadorned, free of all mannerisms and tricks, simple, orderly, clear.

A news story lets the reader know what happened; a feature tells him what it was like to have been there. A news story reports what a person said; a feature, what sort of person said it. A news story tells what the situation is; a feature, how it got that way.

Those tasks are difficult enough. They become nigh impossible if the writer lets his cleverness get in his way. Sometimes we become enamored of a nicely turned phrase, a flash of brilliance over a third bourbon. We scribble it on the doily, rush to the typewriter and try to work the phrase into the story, and try and try.

Give up. The thought must come first, then the poetry. Preconceived cleverness intrudes, breaks up the cadence, does nothing for clarity because in a good feature story every word must tell. Cuteness for cuteness' sake is as obvious as a chorus girl leaping out of the line to demonstrate that she can also pirouette.

Observation Two, related to the first, is that no feature story can ever be more than the material in it. Among the newspapermen I know the best reporters are the feature writers. No one who has written features successfully ever feels he knows enough about his subject. He does know how terribly much sand he must sift to find the nuggets he needs.

Observation Three follows from the other two. It is that both editors and writers are inclined to expect too much of a feature. There are limits to what five-hundred words can do, or five-thousand.

Editors get jumpy, and writers paranoic, during a story's gestation period, which inevitably is longer than the former thinks it ought to be and the latter wishes it were. As time drags, both begin to anticipate more from the unborn story than was ever conceived. The editor burdens his ulcer with unwarranted expectation and the writer clogs his mind with unwarranted guilt. Neither suffers as much as the story.

It would help both to realize early on that no newspaper feature story will ever be the definitive work on any subject; that's not the feature writer's job.

His job is to part the curtain just enough to give the reader a close, penetrating look at one part of the stage. If he chooses his details carefully enough and examines them skillfully enough he surely will suggest what the rest of the stage looks like, but that ought never to be his immediate aim.

I don't know what others understand by that tired phrase, writing in depth, but that is what I take it to mean. To attempt in a feature story to examine the whole crowded stage, as well as the wings and the flies and the orchestra pit, is not to write in depth but in width. Wide writing is cluttered, gutless and dull.

We must pick manageable limits and stay within them. That

means the story must follow a plan. The writer doesn't have to work from a detailed blueprint but he must know in advance all the parts of his story and how they will connect. Even writing that seems impetuous or spontaneous, if it's any good, has a plan.

The feature writer must be able to see his finished story as he sees a river from the window of an airplane. It must flow from precisely here to precisely there and stay within definite banks. It may turn and twist, widen and narrow, rush and slow down, but there must be both logic and symmetry to it. It may not flow recklessly or at random. One traveling the river in a canoe should discover this as he goes along and be ever curious about what lies beyond the next bend.

A reader must also be a discoverer if he would read on. Better not tell him too much or you'll lose him. Tell him the small specific and let him discover the large generality. Tell him the bishop kicked the wastebasket and slammed the door and never mind telling him what frame of mind the bishop was in. Tell him that the widowed farmer braided his daughter's hair with dirt-stained hands and that the child wept in the night—just that, and there will be no need for labored abstractions about the agony and sorrow that attend a mother's death.

During the racial disorders in St. Augustine, Florida, in 1964, a story described a group of participants as "Southern toughs." Terse, yes, but also lifeless. Another story described the same people as "sun-burnished youths in soiled undershirts and work boots waving 25-cent Confederate flags." The second writer let the reader discover for himself what sort of people they were.

A feature writer deals not just in facts and details but in factual subtleties, sensations and emotions that give meaning to facts. He can never stand aloof from his story but must immerse himself in it so that he also feels what he sees and hears. He learns to distrust emotions carefully written down in his note pad and to trust the ones he had when he was too preoccupied by the experience of them to note them down. He needn't worry about recalling them when he gets to the typewriter. He will.

A writer also knows that the chance of being fully understood by every reader is never better than fair, and that finding just the right combination of words and tones and rhythms to say what he means with precision and clarity and taste is the hardest task he will ever have. He approaches the typewriter as an enemy and searches for any excuse to avoid joining the battle. He must do his job alone. There is no one who can help, and he has done the job often enough to know that it never becomes easier. It is always laborious, lonely, and slow.

It is an exquisite form of self-torture that causes the writer to wonder at times why he does it. He knows why. He does it because he knows, is absolutely certain, that when the story is finally written and he asks himself whether the ordeal was worth it the answer will be yes, of course.

Sid Moody

SID MOODY, a prolific writer, is the supervising editor of AP Newsfeatures, a specialized department of The Associated Press that maintains a staff of widely traveled men and women journalists who explore current news situations and personalities in depth. Moody has won numerous prizes for writing and has a long list of story credits including: Writer on the AP books *The Torch is Passed* and *Lightning Out of Israel;* editor-writer on *Triumph and Tragedy;* co-author of *The Lingering Shadow,* a long study of the twenty-six-volume Warren Commission report on the assassination of President Kennedy and on the critics of the report, and of *The USS Pueblo—The Ship That Went Out In the Cold,* a 47,000-word Newsfeature series. Moody is a yachtsman and a reporting expert on the classic America's Cup races.

Serendipity of Feature Writing

BY SID MOODY

Scratch a journalist in almost any anthology and he'll tell you he got there because he wanted to be a newsman ever since he pedaled papers around on his bike or edited his college lit magazine.

All I ever pedaled around as a kid was the *Saturday Evening Post,* and you know what happened to that. My only distinguishing achievement in college was the ability to take off my vest without first removing my jacket. Which trick I've forgotten, and you know what's happened to vests, too.

No, you'd have to say I just stumbled into feature writing like a sourdough staggering through a blizzard into a Klondike saloon. It seemed it would be warmer inside.

I brought with me a degree in history (a useful piece of baggage), eighteen months in the insurance game (useless except for the two days in which I read *The Brothers Karamazov*), and a yen to try journalism. Also, I generally scored a hundred on the *Time* Current Affairs Test, and my sister said I wrote good letters.

I made my debut in a New Jersey weekly publishing complex, where I was told: "You'll be doing a little bit of everything—

reporting, editing, selling space. And, oh yes, some proofreading."

Such proofreading! It was devoted mostly to bowling leagues (transpose a score and you were a dead man), weddings (mostly Slavic, and drop a couple of Zs and you were also a dead man) and display ads (transpose a 7 and a 1 as I once did and you started a run on the local A&P by angry housewives demanding the special on 17¢ sirloin). When I wasn't proofreading, I was collating (stuffing newspaper sections together) from 9 P.M. Wednesday until breakfast Thursday, trying to keep up with a 75-year-old woman who could out-collate a four-color rotary press and who generally left me to ponder the uses of a history degree during the long early morning hours after she had finished and gone.

I was laid off because the town's largest industry had a strike and collators had become a payroll luxury. I prowled about other New Jersey weeklies and ultimately found myself employed on one in Flemington, sitting on my first story on the bench where the cream of the nation's press had sat during the mid-1930s trial of the Lindbergh baby kidnap-murderer, Bruno Richard Hauptmann. This trial, however, involved an irate farmer who had fired some birdshot in the general direction of some boys who had been caught eating apples in his orchard. (He got off.)

I had learned touch-typing while rehabilitating my fingers following an attack of polio on a ship in mid-Atlantic during a hurricane, so what remained to be learned about writing was to put ". . . state police said" in the first paragraph on anything likely to be disputed. This became most valuable a few years later when I was night editor on the AP desk in Newark and put "state police said" at the end of a bulletin saying that an atomic missile had just burned up at McGuire Air Force Base and there was a heavy-radiation alert in South Jersey. There wasn't, actually, but state police had said there was, so my job was saved. Anyway, three weeks later I was transferred to AP Newsfeatures (APN) in New York, which shows you what kind of fallout you can get from sending out a false atomic scare (state police said).

My first APN assignment took me to Sheldon, Iowa, where a woman had lifted some two million dollars from her old man's bank. Being a small-town reporter, I felt right at home in Sheldon. I walked around town knocking on doors and chatting. Then I flew home, and wrote the story in a day which was, I thought, the way you wrote features in Flemington, Sheldon or anywhere else. I guess you could say that was the last day of my innocence.

Not that you can't write a full-length feature in a day. With luck and a good architect, maybe you could build Rome in a day. Just don't count on it.

Well, then, if you already have collating and proofreading and typing down pretty well and you've found every place is not Flemington or Sheldon you're ready to learn something about feature writing.

Once upon a time a feature was a story about a lady wrestler who wrote plays and collected cats and had an adjective in it. Then somebody changed the script and invented the term "in-depth" which sometimes translates as "over-your-head" or "at-length." Today features are "meaningful" and tell the reader why something happened or why someone did what he did. They inform the reader broadly. And sometimes also the writer.

For example, the editor says he wants an in-depth takeout—i.e., a roundup story—on the Central Intelligence Agency, where the right hand doesn't even know if there is a left hand, much less what it's doing. Where to begin? Get some books by hook or crook.

One day you're at CIA headquarters. You mention to the agency public information office (PIO) that you can't find a copy of Allen Dulles' study on intelligence and they loan you a copy providing you promise to send it back.

Then when they escort you to the door, the PIOs remind you that you never were there because the CIA never talks to the press so it doesn't have any press personnel. So you say: "Well, since I was never here, you never loaned me a book so I don't have to return it." Then you hop into a cab and speed off.

You talk to congressmen and aides who are of the select few

Serendipity of Feature Writing

who oversee the CIA, you talk to the many more who wish they were. You talk to boosters and knockers of the agency in and out of government. Along the way you hear about a former high official who left the agency and he's not only a priceless source but leads to others. That's the serendipity of feature writing: you start with a few ideas and sources and along the way you pick up many more of both, some of which may change the concept you had at the beginning of the story. Keep an open mind and learn as you go.

When you think you have enough to write a book, it's about time to write a story. One last thing: by now you may have some ideas about the CIA. Go back to some of your best sources and test out your views with them. It's kind of like trying out the wing flaps before you take off and can be a "Good Thing to Know." Then you decide what you're going to say, organize it in an outline, and say it. If the story sounds accurate to you, turn it in and send the Dulles book back to the CIA.

Maybe now you qualify as a "Knowledgeable Person" about the CIA, which means nothing other than your next assignment will be to cover the fight to save the Redwoods or examine the strange, tranquil life of the Amish or take a trip to sea aboard a Norwegian square-rigged sailing ship and you have to join the Norwegian merchant marine to qualify for passage. Which I did and, for all I know, I'm still a yolly yeoman in the Norse navy.

In square-rigged features you keep your eyes open as much as your ears. (And keep your mouth closed: the descendants of Leif the Lucky prefer to subsist on goat cheese.) You are looking for detail, verbs of description instead of adjectives or adverbs. Sure, the helmsman stands at the wheel like a Viking. But he also clamps his lips into a line to keep out the rain, narrows his eyes to gunslits against the wind, stares transfixed as a swami at the compass light. His knuckles are white from the cold and the strain of the helm. He sails on. The reader may have his own idea of what a Viking is, but you're out there in the wet to tell him what this particular Viking did on this particular ship in this particular storm, and if you can't give him specifics, you might as well be dry inside swallowing goat yogurt and reading about the CIA.

What I mean is it's the little things that tell a lot. Saul Pett (article on page 49) once wrote a classic example when he provided an incisive analysis of the workings of the mind of Robert S. McNamara simply by describing how he acted during a dinner interview—judiciously weighing the options of having a second drink or not, evaluating all the factors in selecting between fish or beef and once having made up his mind, never looking back. Some job, and I don't think Pett used the words "mind like a computer" once. He didn't have to.

McNamara, by the way, provides illustration for something else a feature writer might consider if he hasn't already. Since McNamara was a busy man as defense secretary and you have an hour with him, you get right to the point and ask him prepared questions and you don't digress until you have the answers you need from him that only he can provide. This was in pursuit of a boiled-dinner takeout on him and his administration, not a chatty tête-à-tête-with-Pett piece over crackling fire logs. Working up the story required talking to many of his peers—first. Know your target and precisely what you want from him before sitting down with him—last.

Interviewing a subject's peers is akin to CIA-ing. One source leads to another. The anecdotes and a profile gradually emerge and after awhile it's like you're trying to fit in the last pieces of a jigsaw puzzle and finding one really good quote that takes the place of four not-so-hot ones. More serendipity. You talk maybe forty-five minutes with a McNamara peer and he's good and you think that's enough for now and put away the notebook. Quarry and quarrier are now relaxed, and you chat, and now that no one's on stage any more it's all informal and all of a sudden really good stuff. Moral: you may have got what you came for but don't leave in a rush; there may be more.

There are also coast-of-Maine features. Take a seagull flapping into the wind and a woodcarver who only carves eagles and says when asked why: "What else would a man carve?" Take an ancient boatbuilder who never sails on his own products because he'd rather just stand on shore and look at them, they're so lovely, and a man who's lived in Maine all his life except for the moment of birth which occurred just over the border in Portsmouth, New Hampshire, and who is therefore forever a foreigner from "down south." Put them all together. They don't say all there is to say about the coast of Maine, but they say something of it and its people.

Arthur Everett

ARTHUR EVERETT is the AP's preeminent trial reporter and the New York Bureau's number one writer on major stories. He is well known for the little notebook he fills with pertinent facts before setting out to cover a trial or to interview a personality.

Trials, Interviews, Crime

BY ARTHUR EVERETT

There are many facets to reporting and writing a news story. But no single one of them will guarantee success. Organization is important. But organization cannot provide color. Color is important, but not to the point of obscuring essential detail. Facts are important, but if massed together like a school of fish they can make a story bog down. Direct quotes are always desirable—they often reveal more to the reader in one sentence than paraphrasing can do in several paragraphs.

There was a good example at the trial of Sirhan Sirhan for the assassination of Senator Robert F. Kennedy. When the jury had decided the defendant's fate but before it had returned its verdict, chief defense attorney Grant Cooper, his voice quavering, tears in his eyes, told a reporter: "I'll bet you five bucks it's death." How can any writer better tell of a defense lawyer's anxiety, his fear, the hopelessness enveloping him. And he was right. The verdict was death.

So let's agree that there is no pat formula for interweaving detail, organization, color, quotes and the other ingredients of a good news story. One gropes and experiments.

There are, perhaps, a few guidelines. Not every graphic quote will fit in a first paragraph. Try making a second paragraph of the quote, to underline the lead. Often such a quote will provide a headline, where the lead paragraph might not.

Painting a word picture in a broad pattern is usually preferable. The reader doesn't respond too readily to a string of figures or a mass of minutiae, unless they are converted into a picture that brings home to him the impact and import of the news.

A reporter considers himself a wordsmith or he wouldn't be in the business. But there's no reason to be smug about it. The oldest, safest way to make sure an adjective or phrase you fancy is really the one you want is to consult Webster. You'll be amazed at how often you've goofed.

Backgrounding is part of every reporter's preparation. He can't know too much about a person he's sent to interview; now he has the subject face to face for intelligent questioning.

Courtroom backgrounding is vital. You can't raise your hand to interrupt a district attorney who has brought up a certain name or location or date in his questioning of a witness. So it's invaluable in trial reporting to have a small notebook filled in advance with every name, age, date, incident and quote that can be found on the case. You still won't get through a trial without occasionally being caught short on background, but with preparation it won't happen as often as it might.

Another secret of trial reporting is note-taking. The ear gradually becomes attuned, and you'll abandon one unfinished quote to get on to the more important one on its heels. The knack is getting the part that's most essential—it may be only a paragraph, a sentence, a phrase, or a word.

In the defense opening at the Sirhan trial, attorney Emile Zola Berman said: "At the actual moment of the shooting, he was out of contact with reality, in a trance in which he had no voluntary control over his will, his judgment, his feelings or his actions." This statement summed up the whole defense theory and all the rest of the ten-page opening was supplemental. You're on your way if you got no more than the one word "trance." If you got the full quote, you had it made.

Trials, Interviews, Crime   133

But when, as often occurs, a longer, more involved quote is essential to a story, then the real friends in court are the stenographers. Cultivating them provides insurance when you need to flesh out an incomplete quote with the text.

Remember, however, that not everything is quotes. Notes that appear inconsequential at the time you take them may later help you lead up in your story to a courtroom climax.

Reporters use various methods of calling attention to sections of their notes they deem important. One I know uses a multicolor pen, and the color used emphasizes the degree of importance attached to that section of the notes. I use a bold slash of pencil or pen alongside the quote or notation—one slash to call attention to something I may need later, a double slash if it's likely to figure in the lead, a triple slash if it really seems hot. When skimming back through your notes, let's say, for a weekend piece on the trial, the slashes will guide you to the highlights of the proceedings.

In all reporting, sources are vitally important—people who are willing to volunteer information, or to whom you can turn for background or answers to your questions. A reporter who mines a regular beat has an opportunity to build up sources over a period of time.

A trial reporter on an assignment away from home base, involving people he has never met before, doesn't have that opportunity or that amount of time. One idea you might consider is this: In every trial, there are the legal stars of prosecution and defense. They are usually quite accessible to all reporters.

Almost invariably, also, there are the legal spear carriers, the expert on relevant law, the man assigned to watch out for errors that might win a new trial on appeal. These lawyers drift through the background of a case; they are likely to be a bit jealous of the attention lavished on the stars, a bit covetous of the publicity that eludes them.

Try catering to them, seeking background from them, using their names when possible. Often they are incredible fonts of information on the case, even beyond the legal luminaries whom they serve. And if you're the only one who's close to them, they owe no obligation to the other media representatives. What you get from them is quite likely to be yours alone.

The real experts on communications are the AP foreign service reporters. But even in this country, communications can play a factor, especially in the case of trial reporting, when the verdict comes in and speedy transmission is imperative.

In the second Sam Sheppard murder trial in Cleveland in 1967, news service telephones were located in rented quarters about half a block from the courthouse. The trial judge had ruled no press phones could be installed in the courthouse, beyond those regularly available to the Cleveland dailies.

Thirteen years earlier, in the original Sheppard trial, there was a young second banana on the prosecution staff who, in the ensuing years, became a judge. And his courtroom just happened to adjoin the Sheppard retrial courtroom.

Through past contacts, it was possible to prevail upon this judge to let the AP use the telephone in his chambers for the retrial verdict. It speeded things up considerably.

One should prepare for every story, but no one should anticipate any story. To try to do so can be costly. If you decide beforehand what you're going to find in the way of news and how you're going to write it, you can be thrown irretrievably off stride when things work out differently.

An internationally famous supper club singer was appearing in New York when her lover, of equal prominence in his own field, was killed in a plane crash while en route to join her. She vowed to sing that night and a show-must-go-on drama seemed in the works.

She went on, all right, before a packed house, including several tables of newsmen. But on the surface her performance seemed serene, and not too newsworthy. So a reporter drifted back to the kitchen entry where chefs, busboys and waiters stood listening in the semidarkness. One of them was heard to say something to the effect: "Always before she sings with her voice, but tonight she sings with her heart." The sentimental quote was apt, and it was useful.

And there was a famed Metropolitan Opera and Broadway stage star who came down with laryngitis a few hours before a comeback appearance at the Palace theater. On stage that night, she kidded herself and her audience and croaked her way through a show of sorts that won applause for her courage.

But alone with a reporter in her dressing room afterward, she told of all it had meant to her to come back to the big time after years of obscurity, of her determination not to let her illness interfere, and of her fear that she had flopped—which as a matter of fact she hadn't. The story, like so many others, lay behind the scenes.

A southern judge once wrote a reporter after a trial that he had enjoyed his luncheon sessions with newsmen from all over the country who covered the case. He said: "I found myself doing more talking than at any time since the bull sessions back in law school. It must be because you fellows are trained to be good listeners."

A reporter had better be a good listener. Nothing can turn off a news source quicker than a loose-lipped interviewer. The guy, for instance, who likes to get his own opinion across under the guise of questioning. Or the trial reporter who interrupts a session between his colleagues and the lawyers with reminiscences of his own experiences in other cases. Even in periods of seemingly idle chitchat, other reporters may have questions they want answered or wish to listen in the hope of learning something.

So let's make it a rule in reporting to stop, look and listen.

Stop to get all the facts so when you're ready to write or dictate your story, it won't have holes in it.

Look for the unusual angle, for color, for descriptive touches that will bring the scene alive for the reader, as though he were with you on the spot.

And finally, listen, listen, listen; absorb as much knowledge and background as possible. Your story will reflect the depth of your knowledge, or the lack thereof.

There are fairly fixed formats in organizing and writing some stories. It is the exceptions that impart the fascination.

With an exceptional story never hesitate to try a new approach — an offbeat lead, a chronological recital, emphasis on pathos, or a heart-tugging humorous tag line.

In short, as a reporter and as a writer, you just have to play every story by ear. And remember, the better your product strikes your ear, the better it is likely to strike the reader's eye.

Arthur Gavshon

ARTHUR L. GAVSHON has reported British politics and diplomacy for the AP since World War II and covered many summit and foreign ministers conferences—in London, Paris, Geneva, Berlin, Rome, Brussels, Moscow and Bermuda. Gavshon, born in Johannesburg, previously was political correspondent for a group of South African papers.

The Whitehall Story

BY ARTHUR L. GAVSHON

Real power in Britain today is divided, in terms of influential impact, among the Government, the City of London, the Press and Television.

And since the press and telly can effectively reach out directly to an uncommonly receptive and articulate people, over the government (Whitehall) and the London equivalent of Wall Street (called "The City"), the lot of a newsman can be tough if he sets out to be a genuine seeker of politico-diplomatic information.

The British people for a long time have read more newspapers per head than any other people on earth and the TV tube now is ingrained in the life and culture. Yet many uppercrust Britons harbor disrespect and disdain for the press and the other media.

As late as 1829, Sir Walter Scott advised a friend: "Your connection with any newspaper would be a disgrace and a degradation. I would rather sell gin to poor people and poison them that way."

Until the eighteenth century, the reporting of debates in Parliament had been barred as "a notorious breach of privilege." A breakthrough came when *Gentleman's Magazine* hired a memory man to sit through the sessions so that he could relay the proceedings to Dr. Samuel Johnson who, in turn, put the speeches into classical prose.

Such attitudes persist despite the paraphernalia, impact and importance of the twentieth-century communications industry. The situation is not fortuitous.

But, ever resourceful, the British have evolved a compromise process by preserving Parliament—apart from executive government—as the setting for the fun and games of politics. It is packed with the cosmetics, not with the substance, of power in the form of intrigue and gossip and theater. Sometimes it's good theater, too. But Parliament today makes few decisions that count. Once in a while it blows up with anger or indignation or frustration. Its greatest usefulness in my experience has been in the scope it provides for developing relationships with today's members who could be tomorrow's executive and administrative leaders. There are hazards, of course.

One way of being sucked into the machine of diplomacy or politics is to be wined and dined at stately homes. Another way is to be given a category of information on sensitive situations on condition that it cannot be used except for background. Periodically personal judgments have to be made on whether to accept this sort of information at all. Officials sometimes claim publication could or would imperil lives.

In general my inclination has been to refuse unusable information. This has not always won friends among those trying to influence me.

Luck attended my personal introduction to London's diplomatic beat. I was still in (South African) army uniform when I was hired in 1945. Six months later AP London gave me a trial run as a diplomatic reporter. The regular man was covering a Paris peace conference, and his deputy was ill. London after VE-Day was full of news. In my first few weeks a few exclusives came my way. Nobody has told me since when that trial run will end.

One thing the years have taught me is that in most situations someone somewhere sometime will be ready to talk if only to give a balanced version of what is at stake. Another is that there are at least two sides involved. Sometimes middlemen, too.

It is standard AP practice to give all concerned the chance to have their say. But what happens if no one wants to talk? If you have the slightest inkling of what's afoot there is then a ready-made opening to try for information first with one side, then with the other, or perhaps with compromisers, or neutrals.

I learned never to ignore the neutrals. They're the people or nations who hedge their bets by keeping on terms with the contenders. And they're the ones the contenders want to impress. This keeps neutrals well informed.

This technique paid off for the AP in a big way in the leadership crisis that rocked the then ruling Conservative government of Britain in 1963. Four main candidates were in the running to succeed the stricken Harold Macmillan as Prime Minister. All sorts of information and propaganda turned up. Through it all I concentrated on one middleman member of the government who had long been a source of accurate information. He was, moreover, close to Macmillan, who from his sickbed kept inside the power struggle.

Late one night the normally best-informed national newspapers reported confidently that the then deputy premier, R.A. (now Lord) Butler, had won. But someone close to Sir Alec Douglas-Home (the sometime fourteenth Earl) telephoned me at home to say his man was in. I telephoned my neutral cabinet source, who had gone to bed. "It had better be good," he said sleepily. Then he confirmed my information with the greatest emphasis. The story turned out to be a political sensation: Sir Alec was indeed the new P.M.

A neutral source came to my aid in the early stages of the Soviet-Chinese split. The Russians were trying to patch things up with the Yugoslavs. The Yugoslav embassy in Moscow was told by a member of the Soviet Communist Party's Politburo of a passage in a speech made by the then Premier Nikita Khrushchev which asked: "How would you [his Politburo colleagues] like to

The Whitehall Story

wake up one morning and find the Chinese a nuclear power?" After research I was able to report that a major issue in the Moscow-Peking split was Russia's refusal to share nuclear weapon secrets with the Chinese. Months later Khrushchev publicly confirmed this.

In London there are nearly one hundred diplomatic missions, each with its own interests, its own sources, its own lines of communication. Some diplomats feel lonely, isolated, out of their depth. They appreciate the chance to swap ideas, even information, with London-based people. I make a habit of keeping in close contact with the key missions. Third secretaries I met twenty years before occasionally have returned as ambassadors. I became close friends with one first secretary who today is the most important official adviser to the Prime Minister of his important homeland. We lunch or dine together whenever he is in London.

In today's world of twilight truths and shadowy facts the political–diplomatic reporter must learn quickly whether he is being told something or sold something. I have fashioned a rule that rarely fails to enable me to assess my new informant and, of course, his information: Never ask a test question of substance unless you know the answer.

This calls for self-discipline. Some newsmen like to write their stories aloud or to convey an impression of being well informed by asking too many questions, especially at news conferences.

British newsmen normally hunt in packs. It seems to suit them. It certainly suits the government, which also encourages foreign correspondents to band together in groups for background briefings. This reduces chances for exclusives.

The Foreign Office, which sets the pace in press relations, likes things this way. It runs a daily, open news conference around noon that rarely produces a major story unless the government is ready with some announcement. The real work begins in the afternoon. Groups of noncompeting newspaper representatives meet with individual officials, sometimes ministers. The Foreign Secretary periodically receives the British national diplomatic correspondents en masse, but rarely receives foreign correspondents. Similarly groups of American, West German, French and other special correspondents get together once or twice weekly for special briefings. The Prime Minister's office runs a similar system.

Working on my own has given greater freedom. The London bureau of The Associated Press imposes no limits on my beat. I am accountable only to my office and to the confidences of my sources.

This occasionally has led to bizarre situations. Late one night I was telephoned from 10 Downing Street by a member of the government who asked me, as a favor, to hustle down at once.

It was around midnight when I was ushered into the study of the Prime Minister. Over scotch and soda he told me there had been suggestions that a story I had written had come to me from the minister who had just telephoned me. The minister denied this, quite properly and correctly. But he had been so upset by the suspicions that he had handed in his resignation. The Prime Minister did not inquire as to my source but asked assurance that the minister concerned was not involved. I was able to give that assurance and as a result the British leader tore up his colleague's letter of resignation in my presence.

How does one get to know and keep good sources? It's a long story. In my case a big part of the answer lies in the AP policy of continuity. Over the years, though based in one capital, I have got to know hundreds of diplomats and officials in this and many other countries.

Some of the men I have met have risen to senior status. Some raw lawmakers have become cabinet ministers and then premiers. When Labor ruled after the war I made a point of getting to know up-and-coming Conservatives. Conversely, I did the same after 1951 with the Laborites when they were in the wilderness until 1964.

It's essential to remember that in Britain's stable and democratic scheme of things the changing of the guard does not produce too great an upheaval. When a new government takes over perhaps one hundred or so newcomers move into Whitehall, but

The Whitehall Story

thousands of civil servants stay put. And they are the ones with the real national secrets. Even a new premier cannot get at the files of his predecessors, which are guarded by the permanent officials.

Few political and diplomatic correspondents work a regular eight-hour day and five-day week on our side of the Atlantic. A correspondent lives his job. Night and day. The vital conference might reach its crucial decisions around dawn. Parliament sometimes sits all night. Diplomatic dinner parties often drone on deep into the early hours. So, like a doctor, you're never really off duty.

That takes physical stamina.

But intellectual stamina is needed too.

The weighty government statement suddenly thrust on you has to be digested, understood, interpreted and simplified (but not oversimplified) in a matter of minutes. A wrong verb, an imprecise adjective, an absent qualification or attribution could make big trouble.

Avoidance of the headline easily won with an exaggerated story is not your only worry. You must be concerned in the end with your obligations to accuracy built upon a precise understanding of your sources and perspectives.

George Cornell

GEORGE W. CORNELL writes two weekly columns, "Religion Today" and "Religion in the News," and covers spot news of religion. He has reported assemblies of the national and world councils of churches, the second Vatican Council in Rome, and the visits of Pope Paul VI to the Holy Land, India and New York. His three books are *They Knew Jesus, The Way and Its Ways,* and *Voyage of Faith.*

Updated Religion Reporting

BY GEORGE W. CORNELL

In the last twenty years or so an old pseudo-pious approach to reporting on religion has been discarded, thanks to many of the sources of information and the writers on the subject. This offers greater opportunities to religion writers and it imposes bigger responsibilities on them.

The press often in the past has been blamed, or credited, for influence on the courses of politics, on war and peace, on fashions, on the stock market. Under new ground rules generally accepted with enthusiasm by religion sources and writers, the press also may be held accountable for man's eventual salvation or damnation!

Disciplines of religion writing are equated in an accepted sense now with those of political writing, and neither side need feel downgraded. Consider the high diplomacy and politics of the mid-twentieth century ecumenical movement, for instance.

Reporting of religion especially demands care and precision. It must be done soundly. This is the extra onus taken on by American journalism in moving into forthright coverage of religion.

The situation reminds me of a quote from poet-playwright

Christopher Fry: "Affairs are now soul size. The enterprise is exploration into God."

The job might seem to invite palpitations and penance, but the more appropriate response, in my estimate, involves instead those same qualities called forth for reliable reporting in any news field: an open, inquiring mind, a sensitive ear and eye, and a conscientious determination to find and convey the realities of the subject. The religion reporter is not a booster, not a promoter. Nor is he a critic or a cynic. He is professionally the constant inquirer, looking, hunting for values, meanings, answers, surprises, the nub of the matter which sources in his field have to offer, the untold aspects, the glimmers of the new.

The modern approach to religion reporting is freer, fuller, and more rigorous, candid and probing than the old. Newsmen used to deal rather timidly and superficially with religion, as if it had a fragile, untouchable element about it, not to be subjected to hard news questions and demands for motivations, explanations and objectives.

In my view, there is no facet of religion, however controversial or disturbing to institutions or individuals, that cannot be dealt with in the news if it is done fairly and in perspective. The field rocks with conflict. It always has. It is loaded with tensions, diversities, debate, and the sparks fly often from the theological workshops. One of religion's distinctive characteristics in contrast is its continuous self-criticism. Rarely in other specialties, among businessmen, lawyers, doctors, psychiatrists, are the tenets of their pursuits subjected to such wide-open intramural criticism and contention. But this is the way religion reaches for greater understanding, and if the field is to be genuinely reported at all this crossfire of ideas and methods must be openly handled in the news.

Generally the issues are quite subtle, often peripheral, and the reporter must make sure he understands what is being claimed and what isn't and make both clear when he writes it.

I recall an opinion survey that found a large proportion of seminary students did not believe in man's immortality. The re-

Updated Religion Reporting

searchers assumed this indicated a departure from traditional teachings. Actually, the opposite was the case. Classic church theology always has taught that man was mortal, subject to death, unable in his natural creaturehood to surmount it by his own means without Divine Grace. The students simply were reflecting their doctrinal acuity in the face of a ham-handed survey question.

A related point that must be kept in mind is the considerable amount of theological naïveté that exists. Terms and concepts need to be explained, in simple words, if the meanings aren't obvious. This is especially necessary in the religious field, even though it might seem on the surface that readers interested in religion would know its vocabulary. The fact is that many don't.

The contemporary population is highly informed in many ways, but for many adults religious schooling extended little beyond the childhood level.

Polls have suggested that even a good many college graduates conclude that the Epistles were wives of the Apostles and that from Dan to Beersheba refers to a lovers' exchange. At another extreme, a writer would draw a complete blank if he quoted some Scriptural exegete on a sentence like this: "In the hermaneutics of heilsgeschichte, the kairos of the incarnation inaugurates a koinonia of didache and kerygma which points escatologically to the parousia."

Translated from the theological textbooks to news language, the sentence goes: "In the scholarly interpretation of the Biblical story of man's salvation, the timing of the birth of Jesus inaugurates a community of service and teaching that points finally to the triumph of goodness at the end of history."

Even the ponderous tone of the latter version reminds me that religion reporting should shun any aura of sanctimoniousness. The prose should be hard, specific, in the human vein, rather than in the oracular usages common in the ecclesiastical world. Churches have a way of over-exercising cultish terms such as "apostolate," "stewardship," "undergird," "witness." These are simple enough in themselves but they are not the way people talk or the way we should write.

Perhaps the number one point to remember in religion reporting is that you are dealing with religion, which by definition involves mystery, the unknown, wonderment. It is not just hard facts—names, numbers, organizational clanking.

We should consistently bear in mind the different approaches to faith by the different groups. Few religious stories in this heterogeneous country can be told well simply from the view of a fractional segment of it. That view must be related—put in perspective. Because the subject of religion is not included in general education, most teaching about it takes place in separate denominational compartments. This results in a great deal of mutual ignorance and misunderstanding among the different groups, despite the tempering effect of the modern ecumenical movement. Consequently, in a news story, you've got to bridge tribal chasms of inadequate information or misinformation.

The ramifications of most religious stories of any significance almost invariably go beyond any one denominational grouping. You may hear about a development in one group, but a little checking will bring out that the same or similar considerations and problems are current elsewhere, and a more complete account will include the full range of the matter. In this age of heavy cross communications, the isolated happening is rather rare.

As an intellectual-psychic-ethical system, religion has implications in nearly every area of human activity and its moral-spiritual reckonings of events and circumstances can be sought out and reported. This usually involves checking with a number of ethicists in the area involved. And the possibilities are always there for bringing out that side of a situation, whether it's a bombing, a race riot, a foreign-aid bill, a hanging, or the Middle East.

Judging from the reaction I get, I'm convinced that stories dealing with basic concepts, with inquiries into and convictions about the basic meanings and purposes of life, are of general interest to people. They'll read other stories about the politics and programs of the religious organizations, the oiling, cranking and repairing of the machinery and personnel. But as indicated by my

Updated Religion Reporting 149

mail, they are far more concerned with, and read more avidly, those stories involving doctrines and views exploring the fundamental premises and possibilities of life.

This sort of story often involves more questions than it does final answers, but this condition seems to be part of the makeup of our species.

JOHN CUNNIFF writes the AP daily *Business Mirror,* a column appearing in hundreds of newspapers five days a week with stories that can't be told in dollar signs. He figures that in four years he has turned out 700,000 columnar words at a rate of about 500 per day for the AP wires. Cunniff was born in Boston, educated at Boston University and Columbia and had wide experience as a news and feature reporter, writer and editor before taking over the column. He won the George Polk Memorial Award of Long Island University in 1961 for research and reporting on the plight of Tennessee tenant farmers, and he has lectured widely. His wife writes a personal finance column under her maiden name, Anne Taylor.

Business News

BY JOHN CUNNIFF

Among the truths revealed to successful business editor-writers in their rare but enlightening encounters with the educational process is that unlearning can be as important as learning. Bad habits plague this craft as well as any other. Golfers forever strive to drive across water hazards when they know that economically they should play it short. Cab drivers, without regard for their own economy, run red lights when they know they could get tickets or lose jobs.

Bad habits hang around like parasites wherever they are fed by repetition and made to feel at home by people doing what they never intended to do, or never knew they did, or didn't want to do, or knew shouldn't be done. There is a sound economy of purpose lost somewhere in the process.

Bad habits have found a home in business writing. Ask a business news writer why he writes obvoluted prose when clear, concise sentences would do the job better, why he persists in using the jargon of the financial community when only one in every 50,000 of his audience is a financier, why he waits for a business to make announcements and then accepts them uncritically instead of going out after the news. You'll get some fancy answers but you shouldn't accept them. You'll recognize them as bad habits, misconceptions.

We all fight to retain concepts which have become familiar to us, giving them a home in our heads when, if evaluated for substance, they might prove unworthy even of our acquaintance. An incorrect assumption is intellectual soot lodged in the channels of the brain—blocking, clogging, diverting.

In business news writing the biggest piece of soot, the primary misconception, is the notion that there is something extraordinarily special about any story in which numerals and dollar signs are used. Some reporters and writers freeze at their sight, and so the language also becomes frozen. Deserving of meat and potatoes, the reader is served a cake of ice instead.

Let me illustrate:

The scene is a news conference, the first in eighteen years by Smalltown Belt & Bolt Co., for nearly a century the town's biggest employer. Smalltown is fighting a takeover attempt by Fastgrowth Inc., formed three years ago in Bigtown by a "brilliant" twenty-eight-year old entrepreneur. Fastgrowth knows that Smalltown is cash rich and ripe for plucking, and so it has solicited shares from owners at a price well above the market. Now the old management is fighting for its life. At the microphone is an aged gentleman, flushed and agitated.

"As Smalltown's chairman and chief executive officer," he begins in a quavering voice, "I denounce this brazen attack on our company.

"It isn't only this firm that must be defended. We must also preserve a ninety-year tradition. We must save this city. If this unprincipled attack by these upstart out-of-towners succeeds it will mean hundreds of jobs lost in our community. We must not let it happen.

"Our attorneys have advised me that highly irregular procedures are being used by our opponents to solicit shares, and we must warn them that any violation of our rights will be met with an immediate legal response."

That was the scene.

This is one reporter's story: "Millsville (Special)—Smalltown

Belt & Bolt Co. announced today. . ." Let's stop there. Why read on? We've all seen announcement stories, and as quickly as we can turn a page we classify them with the social news.

That is not to say that there is nothing different about financial stories. There is. Some restrictions are set by the material. How, for instance, can you tell your readers that Smalltown declared its regular fifty-cent dividend except by writing it that way? Try to be creative about that one and you'll receive the angriest letters that disturbed stockholders can write.

The same is true of some other stories, especially about corporate income reports and those that concern the stock, bond and commodity markets. These are repeat stories, fixtures. Often the audience is special and is capable of putting the facts into perspective on its own.

But those are purely financial stories. Why do writers insist on giving the same treatment to the drama of the entire business scene? Shouldn't the social and cultural phenomena of men and women hoping and working and producing and failing and succeeding and moving the country be treated with more imagination? A computer can do an adequate job on financial news, and a computer is an utterly unimaginative robot. If that's the way business writers view themselves, they had better watch out. The computer is much faster and not nearly as prone to error.

There is, I'll concede, something special about the way the business writer prepares for and researches an assignment. He must realize that his job is to translate the activities of specialists for a readership of generalists. He must educate himself about financial matters without becoming a financier. He must study hard and he must maintain files, because business events have long histories and no one mind can retain all the details. He must understand the operations of government agencies, because the volume and importance of business news coming out of Washington is growing all the time.

When he sits down to write, however, he must use the same English language used by any good reporter.

But some readers suggest that a business writer must be more careful than others in his choice of words, because an error or

John Cunniff. One aim is to eschew arcane language in a daily column translating the doings of the business world for the average reader. Above, he stands outside the New York Stock Exchange.

misinterpretation may cost people money. That's an argument I hope I'll never hear again. An error in any story may cost the reader the truth, and no dollar value can be placed on that. If writers use vague language and clichés merely because they don't understand the hard, factual truth, then they are kidding themselves and abusing the reader.

Nevertheless, anyone who has edited business news copy has

had the frustrating experience of seeing young writers enter the field with fresh, uncorrupted styles but lapse within two months into writing announcement stories. Which brings me back to the Smalltown news conference:

What happened to that newsman's instincts for recognizing a good story? Wasn't there enough contrast between young and old, small company against large, big city versus small, the possible loss of jobs, the life-death struggle, the threatened legal action, the suggestion of impropriety to build more than just an announcement?

That reporter would have done better to thaw out, become a bit irreverent toward the institutions and the titles involved and a bit more open to the social-cultural-financial adventure unfolding before his eyes.

For the best business news stories aren't that at all; they're simply good stories. If writers try to make their reports fit the old ill-conceived notions they will ruin them. That little despot dollar sign should not dictate to the writer. He should shoot it down.

FENTON WHEELER, AP bureau chief in Madrid, was the only American resident news correspondent in Cuba from February, 1967, until his office was closed by Castro in September, 1969. He and his wife specialized in Latin American studies, working and traveling in Mexico, Chile, Argentina, Brazil, Uruguay and Puerto Rico, before going to Cuba as an AP news and photo team.

Covering Castro's Cuba

BY FENTON WHEELER

I spent two years, seven months and almost twenty-six days reporting in Cuba. Then came a telephone call from the Foreign Ministry at 3 A.M. September 8, 1969. Three hours later my wife and I were sitting in a security room at José Marti International Airport waiting to be expelled.

Covering Cuba had reduced itself to two basics, both difficult: obtaining accurate information and getting it out of Cuba. Everything else was an exercise in futility—and training for the next round.

Newly arrived journalists, accustomed to an information office, to contacts with government officials, and to just asking questions wherever and whenever they want to, normally reached a state of perplexity in about forty-eight hours.

"What do you do to get news in Cuba? I can't find anyone official to talk to. As a matter of fact I can't even find anyone in his office," said a new arrival after circling Havana for two days.

As the only regularly assigned news correspondent from the United States in Cuba, I found it just as tough. It was not easy for any correspondent, even those from "friendly" countries.

Covering Cuba took perseverance, tact, careful checking of facts, patience and a lot of questions.

Ask any question of anybody, said the Foreign Ministry. But many questions were considered "provocative" and with them went a reputation that often cut the tenuous lines to official sources.

Irritating bureaucrats and stupid replies were part of the daily routine. Often the results of hours of work ended up in the wastebasket. But the challenges seemed to justify the effort.

There were lighter moments: People at the Czechoslovak embassy in Havana celebrating their national day (before the August, 1968, Soviet invasion of Prague), demanding Polish vodka and singing *"Deep in the Heart of Texas"* . . . A Cuban national tourist official telling me I could not cancel my hotel reservation because it had not been confirmed.

There was no more physical danger than in other foreign posts. Cubans are lively and good company. Professionally, it was a difficult assignment.

Cuba has no formal censorship. But Communist party readers watched outgoing dispatches closely and a sensitive paragraph could bring a delay of hours or days. It could also bring a call from the Foreign Ministry press section, which probably would contend the story was not objective but would not demand that it be killed.

The idea that someone was reading over your shoulder was not pleasant. Especially when it might be Prime Minister Castro. I asked a Foreign Ministry press aide if Castro read the dispatches from Havana. "You can bet he does," the aide replied.

As The Associated Press correspondent and an American in Cuba I was considered from the very outset as part CIA agent, part Pentagon representative and part mouthpiece for the State Department. Nothing was further from the truth.

But Castro's haranguing over the years had taken its toll. A transportation ministry official once told me, "We don't give news to imperialist agencies." My question to him had concerned the number of injured in a train crash. The death toll had been officially announced hours earlier.

Yet, the official Communist party newspaper *Granma* published some of my dispatches when they considered them favorable. The national radio one day took an AP Havana story, saying Cuba had more doctors than before Castro, and broadcast it hourly.

The uncomfortable moments were more frequent: When Castro attacked me in a speech and the national newsreels played it back for a week. Or attending a meeting and having cameras pointed at me as the speaker denounced "imperialist news agencies."

Western correspondents—or at least I—developed a routine when the crowd was on its feet shouting for Yankee blood. I timed the applause, wrote down the chants and watched the banners wave.

Cuban officialdom normally was polite, if firm. At times it went beyond its official responsibilities to be kind. My wife received almost royal treatment when she visited a kindergarten unannounced. I attended a trial and was taken later to a non-public trial while a citizen-judge slowly and painstakingly explained the procedure to me point by point.

Most AP copy was sent direct by Western Union cable to the office in New York. The cable office in Havana, like many Castro government offices, frequently was undermanned because some of the staff were detached to work in agriculture. That, plus the fact that the equipment was old, provided a handy excuse for the government to say cables had been delayed by technical problems.

A Western Union employe called me aside shortly after my arrival and said: "Wheeler, don't believe anything we tell you. If you call up and ask when your cables left, we will give you a time, but it means nothing." It was an understatement.

At times I dictated urgent news dispatches by telephone. Phone calls to the United States mainland normally cannot originate in Cuba but U.S. calls can be received. So telephoning took some planning ahead. On all Castro speeches, for example, I asked by cable for the New York Foreign Desk to phone Havana at an hour I estimated the speech would have produced something. Then I stewed until the call came in.

In emergencies, I called Mexico, Puerto Rico and, one time on the off chance, Baltimore, to report a hijacking.

I had picked Baltimore because I knew of an NBC newsman

who a few months earlier had placed a call to his wife there that had gone through.

My call did, too, direct from my apartment to the home of the AP's Baltimore bureau chief, whose thirteen-year-old daughter, cool and quick, took my dictation letter-perfect. Fifteen minutes later the story was on the AP wires in the United States and abroad.

Photo telephone calls to transmit Wirephotos were a constant headache. The government, in effect, censored these by requiring The Associated Press to apply for permission to send them, plus a description of the photo and its caption lines. It also limited the number.

Technically, personnel from the Foreign Ministry press section were supposed to check caption lines in the AP office. But they seldom did. This confidence, if that is what it was, was not misplaced. No Wirephoto during my stay was sent from Cuba without government permission.

Even with approval, transmission was sticky. The Foreign Ministry press section was responsible for informing the telephone company in advance that The Associated Press planned to send a photo on our direct line to New York. Calls repeatedly were broken in the middle of a picture—or never came. Once, I was told our line was busy—while I was looking squarely at the telephone with the receiver on the hook.

Mail provided another way to send stories out. Also, I sent by a special routing because regular service between Cuba and the outside was uncertain and painfully slow. Both Cuban and U.S. regulations were to blame.

Despite these problems, Cuba was not the grim scene many people imagine. Nobody followed journalists regularly, at least not in my time. A correspondent could talk to anybody who would talk to him.

I could go as far out of Havana as my gasoline would take me. Because of rationing, however, and because it was not a good idea to show up hundreds of miles from Havana without having told somebody official, I cleared long trips through the Foreign

Fenton Wheeler. He is among the few Americans who reported Castro's Cuba from the inside and who, like the others, was eventually expelled.

Ministry. The ministry provided extra gasoline and offered a guide. It also arranged for a correspondent to see projects he otherwise might have been prohibited from viewing. The one rule of thumb I always followed was to steer clear of military installations lest suspicions of spying be raised.

When my wife and I first arrived in Cuba in 1967, we took a nine-day, unescorted trip of the island. This was before gasoline rationing and guides.

Some of the tabus, like rules enforced by bureaucrats anywhere, were ridiculous. I was prohibited from taking photographs of the presidential palace, a graveyard of old cars, a funeral procession and a militiaman on guard duty. But two days later I could have photographed the same things.

The news problem in Cuba was, and I suppose will always be, getting factual, accurate information. Officials were reluctant to talk and many times replied that they felt no obligation to speak to an American correspondent.

A primary source for every correspondent was the Communist party newspaper, *Granma,* named after the launch that took Castro from Mexico to Cuba in 1956 to begin his uprising. I read it without fail. This often meant a time-consuming check of what the paper said a week, a month or a year ago. It also meant a look into the AP Havana files. Filing, I found, was a vital part of the job.

I also checked other publications and the provincial newspapers, which were less sophisticated than those of Havana and often got right to the point. The newspaper *Adelante* of Camaguey, for example, ran planting, fertilization and sugar cane cleanup figures that indicated which way the harvest would go before it began.

Speeches by Castro—he is an unquestioned source—were invaluable.

I tapped Eastern and Western diplomatic sources, foreign experts, especially invited visitors, businessmen, students, pro- and anti-Castroites, intellectuals, young Communists, fired officials and ordinary Cubans.

I went directly to the ministry involved in a story although the trip was usually fruitless.

Many times I was deliberately fed misinformation. Near the end of the tour it became evident almost by the hour that Castro didn't give a damn for conventional news media, especially those with headquarters in the United States.

A pretty girl from the Young Communist League admitted defiantly that the government did not always tell the truth.

"Why should it? The imperialist agencies don't," she said.

My wife, who sat in with me on all Castro speeches when she was not at the scene with a camera, helped immeasurably on the social side.

We attended as many official and cultural functions as possible. You could never tell when you would bump into Castro or a key minister.

Covering Castro's Cuba

Periodically I asked Castro for an interview. The requests were never acknowledged. Once in a post-speech rainstorm I spoke to him briefly. The area was too jammed for me to reach my fountain pen, and the note paper long before had become mush.

No one from The Associated Press office except my wife, accredited as a photographer, and I sent out stories.

The Cuban staff was loyal and hard-working but I learned quickly their position could not be compromised by asking them to do things that would seem natural elsewhere. This frequently meant I had to sign papers or appear in person to handle routine office housekeeping chores. I was my own accountant, my own banker, my own treasurer, my own administrator and my own editor.

After two and one half years, the whole thing was wrapped up in a two-minute session at 4 A.M. in the Foreign Ministry.

"You have two hours to get to the airport," said the head of the foreign press section. There was no explanation, and nothing left to say but, "Thanks."

When JOHN RODERICK talked with Mao Tse-tung in 1947, the Chinese chairman and his Communist forces were in Yenan, a jump ahead of the pursuing Nationalists of Chiang Kai-shek. Nevertheless, Mao confidently invited Roderick to visit him two years later in Peking. Mao's peripatetic revolution triumphed and he made it to Peking but Roderick is still trying to get there to see Mao. Like other American correspondents, Roderick was stymied by the impasse between Peking and Washington. So old China hand Roderick became a new breed of China Watcher on the Red periphery, based in Tokyo and occasionally Hong Kong.

The China Watchers

BY JOHN RODERICK

The ancient Chinese had a wit and brevity that charmed the eye and titillated the mind. An example: "Of thirty-six ways to escape, the best is to run away."

In eleven words, this tells volumes about the Chinese.

The Chinese Communist descendants of such pithy phrase-makers as Confucius and Lao-tse are, by comparison, verbose, trite and humorless. Called on to say the same thing, they would write 1,000 words condemning the idea of escape as anti-Marxist, anti-party and—in an oft-repeated cliché—"a rotten trick of U.S. imperialism and Soviet revisionism."

Somewhere in the dense undergrowth, smothered by quotations from Chairman Mao Tse-tung, they might indirectly reveal a bit of hard news: a minister cashiered, a general promoted.

Not all the Chinese Communists are fuzzy. Mao himself has a lively, pungent style. So does Foreign Minister Chen Yi. Lin Piao, Mao's designated successor, told the country's writers and bureaucrats: "Don't write those stinking, lengthy and dry articles. They are like machine-made things devoid of sentiment and uninteresting."

But despite these injunctions, Chinese prose continues to be leaden and often next to incomprehensible. China's leaders are for the most part former peasants and soldiers—good at the heady business of revolution but ignorant of the niceties of written logic. To be politically safe, they indulge in double-talk while parroting the pious Marxist-Leninist thoughts of Mao and Lin.

The jungle of bureaucratic Chinese rhetoric stands as a major challenge to newsmen trying to tell the often murky story of China today.

Readers who subscribe to the conviction that the world's history moves in twenty-four hour cycles, broken down into morning papers and evening papers, understandably want to know what is happening in China each day. A staff of Associated Press correspondents in Tokyo and Hong Kong, among them bilingual Chinese and Japanese long-trained to the task, devote themselves to this daunting assignment. They are the generally unsung "China reporters," hunched over the Hsinhua (New China news agency) teleprinters, glued to the monitored reports of the mainland's radios, ready with pencil and paper to interview any returning traveler.

They get the news and relay it speedily: A bloody battle among Maoists, a Chou En-lai speech, the election of a revolutionary committee. The demands of time and space limit the backgrounding and interpretation they can do.

Important though it is, daily coverage of China forms only a small part of the whole. To flesh out these factual bones, The Associated Press produces analyses, backgrounders, special reports, profiles and features. Most of them are the end result of a new approach—scholars describe it as a discipline—called China Watching.

The China Watcher is a journalist, a scholar or a diplomat who hacks his way through the wordy Chinese forest in sometimes vain pursuit of the clear, but hidden, fields of deeper understanding. Sifting, analyzing, checking his memory and his files, consulting the history, culture and philosophy of China, he employs a technique that might earn a "Well done, old fellow," from Sherlock Holmes.

The materials he uses are neither secret nor exotic. They in-

John Roderick. The AP correspondent shown in a meeting with Mao Tse-tung (right) nearly a quarter century ago, before Mao's Communists seized power in China. "Meet me in Peking," Mao prophetically invited Roderick....

clude the daily transmissions of Hsinhua, the broadcasts of mainland radios, the translations of Western diplomatic establishments, issues of *Red Flag,* the *Peking People's Daily,* the *Liberation Army Daily,* the *Peking Review, China Reconstructs,* and *China Pictorial,* the dispatches of Japanese, Yugoslav, Polish, Russian and Romanian correspondents in Peking, as well as the government intelligence made available from Washington, London and Vienna.

This is a mass of information—and sometimes misinformation—that must be approached gingerly; no single fact will yield the big picture the China Watcher wishes to paint.

This writer's own method is to clip and file what becomes available, to make mental notes of apparently trivial events reported in the official press, to talk with whatever experts are at hand, and then to read.

Reading can be voluminous: in addition to the many routine sources it may involve digging back ten years in files to corroborate a hunch, reading an armful of books for evidence of the impact of the past on the leaders of the Chinese present.

Long-forgotten speeches suddenly endowed with new meanings, old writings now said to apply to the passionate present, official histories, documents, biographies, newspaper articles, "I-have-been-there" books by the knowledgeable and the gulled: all need to be dipped into, pored over, culled.

The reading done, a new search begins for the human factor that will bring greater life to the work under way: a returned traveler, tourist, diplomat or author. Locating them is not easy. The comings and goings on the mainland are less frequent than before. Once found, the narrow knowledge they can offer often adds little of value.

The material and notes gathered on the writer's desk for a China project usually overflow one, sometimes two desks in the Tokyo bureau. Putting them together is an exercise in alertness (Chinese propaganda has soporific qualities), persistence and a touch of clairvoyance. A devotion to *Alice in Wonderland* helps, and of course the clouded crystal ball.

Before 1962, China Watchers groped in almost unrelieved darkness. Their chief asset was an ability nurtured over the years to read between the lines of Chinese propaganda. By substituting "Soviet Russia" in Chinese attacks on Yugoslavia, and "China" in Soviet denouncements of Albania, it was possible to affirm as early as 1957 that the Chinese–Soviet break had begun.

The evidence, in the opinion of China Watchers, piled up each month. But it was not until Moscow and Peking publicly admitted it in 1962 that they were really believed. After that, the going was easy as millions of words rolled off the Moscow and Peking presses.

Similarly, signs of an internal Chinese split were hard to come by prior to 1965. By probing and analyzing, this writer was able

The China Watchers

to note that "Communist society is split by cracks and fissures which no one suspected existed" (1958); that Lin Piao was being called Mao's apt pupil and appeared to be moving up (1960); that there appeared to be disaffection in the army (1959). There were other hints that the Great Leap Forward had failed, that the intellectuals were on the warpath, that the cultural purge was about to begin.

After August, 1966, the floodgates of revelation opened and by close check and interpretation the rise of a new elite (Madame Mao, Madame Lin Piao, Chen Po-ta) and the fall of the old (Liu Shao-chi, Teng Hsiao-ping, *et al*) could be fairly predicted.

For the China Watcher a poverty of sources had turned into an embarrassment of riches by 1970. With the cultural revolution all but over, many once fluid sources again began to dry up. The famine in the wake of this feast may well be too much for some China Watchers. Mistakes (they have never been free of them) are bound to occur.

But many would agree that of the thirty-six ways to prophesy which way the Chinese dragon will turn, China Watching is one of the better ones.

William Glover

Drama critic WILLIAM GLOVER covers Broadway—On, Off and Off-Off. He grew up ten minutes from Times Square and became a member of the Critics' New York Drama Desk (vice president), the New York Drama Critics Circle (president 1967-69) and the Players.

The Beat of Broadway

BY WILLIAM GLOVER

The craft of criticism is haunted by odd irony. Admit that is your job and anyone, just anyone, anytime is ready to come back with a snappy: Just who do you think you are?

The question, implying that the veriest aborigine might have been a preferable choice, merely points out that, deep down, willy-nilly, and God help us, no one is immune to the urge to judge, censure, improve and even occasionally admire the deeds of others.

After the primal trinity of survival essentials—food, shelter and sex—are assuaged, *Homo sapiens* always exercises his critical instinct. He invents, he climbs the social ladder, and he otherwise expresses dissatisfaction with past attainments.

And over in that enclave of endeavor, the arts, a poet dreams of a better world, a painter epitomizes terror or beauty, a musician transmutes elusive vision into golden melody. Olympian critics all.

And each, in unstoppable chain reaction, is vulnerable to the response of the public at large and those "sentinels in the avenues of fame," the capital-C Critics.

There is always going to be the standard deviation, a maverick with eccentric and probably egotistical credo, but the vast majority of professional appraisers who attend art galleries, concerts and playhouses approach their chores with a carefully developed philosophy of solid responsibility.

And with one thing more: A total experience of training and exposure that provides standards of value.

Let's particularize with the theater reviewer for a news service. In the course of a Broadway season, he sees about seventy productions. Off-Broadway and Off-Off-Broadway he can take in another seventy or eighty. And because New York no longer is the unchallenged center of theatrical aspiration, he inspects a dozen regional repertory presentations. For balance, periodic visits to drama in Europe are in order.

Add all that up, and about two hundred nights out of three hundred sixty-five are gone. If he's lucky, on about forty evenings the event will justify the anticipatory excitement that somehow always precedes curtain-up. With all their faults, reviewers are the most stagestruck incurables of civilization.

So when you envy the aisle sitter for being the first to see the newest blockbuster, just remember all those numbing disasters his words helped save you from. You won't, but you should.

A perverse imp always perches on the reviewer's midnight typewriter, wondering whether the judgment being pounded out is fair. On a news wire, loaded with fast-breaking events, the problem is intensified.

In a maximum allotment of about four hundred words, critical balance must be struck swiftly—and with awareness that the report has to be equally readable in big city and small town. You just hope that something you say this time will make new converts aware of the pleasures and merits of living theater.

What you can't think about is the effect your opinion may have on those who produced the show you are examining. At least not more than once.

For me, *Cleopatra* provided a traumatic example of what can happen if you think about anything but the event itself.

The forty-million-dollar cinematic opus starring Richard

Burton and Elizabeth Taylor had its first press showing the night before its New York premiere. Under the ground rules, a twenty-four-hour hiatus was required before it could be reported.

The film, my own critical values unanimously agree, was a collossal bore. But for two hours after sitting down to write the review, I couldn't get a single sentence on paper. Then I realized I was suffering journalistic buck-fever.

The reasons, of course, were: the picture was the costliest ever made; the fate of a major film studio was riding on the verdict; and because of all the buildup publicity, this was one story everyone would read—and I didn't know what anyone else thought about it.

The snapout from paralysis came because by the time I got to my office in response to an urgent summons two things had happened: On a fifteen-minute taxi ride the first-paragraph dilemma was solved; and some London papers had broken the embargo, so the deadline for my copy wasn't tonight but right now. The relentlessly moving clock is undoubtedly the curse and blessing of journalism.

Covering the theater doesn't stop with first-nighting. There must also be interviews and background features.

In pursuit of the new and intriguing and possibly true in that sometimes magic land of Broadway, it is possible to:
- Have your ears caressed with champagne
- Confer with a belly dancer on a fire escape.
- Encounter something comparatively exotic in subject and ambiance

With far greater likelihood, it is also possible to:
- Run afoul of a grunter, glarer or flipper
- Find survival contingent on, 1. cajoling pets, 2. ignoring flighty aides, or 3. fending off the flailing fists of some sonny who doesn't want mommy interviewed this afternoon.

Such activities develop a yoga knack for going into coma despite the bawling baby next door or ninth-inning rally on TV; a measure of ability at instant psychoanalysis; and a capacity for gallons of coffee. Others there be who favor headier brews, but the breed is losing ground as the communications race speeds up.

There are also the peculiar tribal customs of opening night to learn and accept with Buddha-like calm. Highly desirable is cultivation of the ability for a broken-field sprint up the aisle to a taxi as the curtain falls.

Legitimate theater bases its excitement on a strange, varied and looney assortment of individuals. A handcraft business in a digital-computer era, its methods are bewildering and devious. More and more, the closer you look.

You soon learn that the bigger the player, the easier he or she is to reach for a story. Glamour dolls from filmland on an excursion into stage acting are the toughest, probably due to insecurity.

There are always exceptions, of course. A musical comedy queen may be out of sorts and turn up for an interview as a glarer. She's put on dark glasses, so your best conversational guides, the eyes, simply vanish. The only rejoinder is for you to put on shades, too.

Then there's the grunter. It could be Noel Coward. As he busies with makeup pencil, every question elicits "yes," "no," or "um." When the notebook closes, he thaws to thank you for the informal interview style. "I've been told that before—usually by elderly actresses," pops the unpremeditated response. After all Katherine Cornell and Eugenie Leontovitch have said such things. But the next time Coward talks.

The flipper could be Peter Ustinov. Every query is tiddly-winked away; amiable, amusing patter but no story. In contrast, the late Tallulah Bankhead once livened up a meeting with the champagne bit, leaning across the sofa to apply a bit of spilled bubble water to the aural lobes "for luck," which you sometimes need on the beat of Broadway.

Bob Thomas

BOB THOMAS' father, George H. Thomas, was a San Diego newspaper editor until he moved to Hollywood to be press agent for Mary Pickford, Thomas Ince and, in due course, most major studios. In addition to columning and reporting, Bob Thomas has written books including biographies of movie magnates Harry Cohn, Irving Thalberg and David O. Selznick.

Hollywood

BY BOB THOMAS

Covering the West Coast entertainment beat was fairly simple when, at age twenty-two, I started writing The Associated Press Hollywood column in 1944. Almost all movie-making was concentrated at eight major studios. Radio had dozens of big stars, and nearly all worked at one or another of the three big networks. The record industry was controlled by five companies.

Today the movie industry is worldwide, television entertainment is produced by a score of companies, and the pop and rock music world stretches from Hollywood to Nashville to Liverpool.

But while the entertainment scene is infinitely more complex, covering it is much the same. The reporter just needs stronger legs.

As with all reporting, you need to be informed. This is especially true in entertainment, where trends and faces change quickly. It pays to read all the trade journals, the movie pages of the newspapers, the national magazines and the gossip columns, to keep up with what is going on. You read, you listen. By dropping in at the studio, attending previews, visiting press receptions and going to industry banquets, you find out what people in the trade are doing and talking about. That can lead to story ideas.

Hollywood

Most of my writing is dependent on generated ideas.

It's one thing to cover hard news; then you must gather the facts and present them in a readable and effective way. It's another thing to have a supply of white space which you have to fill regularly. You are competing for newspaper space with hard news, with all kinds of features, with your own competitors in the same field.

In a sense you are *creating* news—researching and presenting stories that might not have been covered if you hadn't dreamed up the idea. That's the challenge, and that's what makes the Hollywood assignment endlessly interesting.

Most of my ideas for columns come from what interests me. A few are suggested by AP editors or are requested by AP newspapers. Some come from press agents.

Press agents—or publicists, as they prefer to call themselves—are a much-maligned fraternity. In some instances the maligning is warranted, and I've had some wowsers tried on me. But over the years I've heard every press agent's ploy—and besides, my father was one.

The trick is in learning to say no and in using press agents for help. They can be very helpful in letting you know when newsworthy personalities are in town, in making arrangements for interviews, in getting statements from their clients. One of the biggest headaches for a reporter in Hollywood is reaching people. Show folks are peripatetic and have unlisted telephone numbers.

The interview is one of the more delicate forms of human intercourse. Usually in Hollywood there are three persons present —the reporter, his subject, and a press agent. The press agent's presence is not as insidious as it may sound. Only a few times have I heard a press agent caution a star about a statement—usually over something inconsequential. The professional press agents maintain silence, or sometimes they can help by drawing out a shy interviewee. A few stars don't allow press agents to be present. Gregory Peck is one.

I believe that interviews should be conversation—give and take between two individuals. The exchanges are usually friendly but they need not be; you're there to get a story, not to ingratiate. In the past I have tried to conduct the interview without taking notes; I trained myself to record the pertinent quotes in my mind. Sometimes for a long interview or for someone who is especially erudite note-taking is necessary.

My job would be completely enjoyable if I only had to do interviews. Unfortunately I have to write them, too.

Usually I wait until the following day before writing the interview. By then my mind has sifted out the important elements. The lead might come to me in the shower or on the freeway. Beginnings are easy, I find. It's that final sentence that's tough.

Each interview is different. Some stars can be delights. Humphrey Bogart was one. He loved to issue outrageous statements to stir up the film community. "Let's touch a nerve," he'd say.

Some stars have had reputations for poor interviews—Gary Cooper, James Stewart, Fred MacMurray. I never found them unproductive. All much-interviewed personalities, they became bored with the same old questions. But if you got them onto subjects in which they were intensely interested, they would produce.

Covering Hollywood has changed. Many of the fabulous stars have been claimed by death. Changing economics have altered the movie business, and a more enlightened audience has expressed more interest in the business and esthetic aspects of film than in personalities.

As a result, I find myself doing fewer personality interviews and more articles on the trends in film content and business. This requires much digging and inquiring.

There are a few Hollywood stories each year that require fast reporting and writing. Often they are deaths of well-known personalities, and such stories require well-grounded research. The AP bureau in Los Angeles has good files and I maintain my own at home as well. I also have a large library of film and television literature to draw from.

Each year the Academy Awards require fast handling, and

that is one of the challenges of my work. I dictate the story from the place where the awards are held. It helps to have plenty of background on the contenders so you can give the reader more than the bare results. Speed is all-important, since you are competing with the opposition on a split-second basis.

I have been asked, "Don't you get tired of covering the same beat?" The answer is: "Impossible."

It isn't the same beat. When I started out, the movie world was tightly controlled and insular. Today it is exploding, as are all forms of entertainment.

Most of all, the personalities are changing. I began by interviewing Greer Garson and Errol Flynn. Now it's Raquel Welch and Peter Fonda.

About the AP

On any given day, many millions of Americans will get most of their national and international news, printed or broadcast, from The Associated Press. Few will be aware of the fact. AP dispatches are an inseparable part of the newspapers they read or the newscasts they hear.

Yet the AP is a complex and highly individual structure of its own. It is the oldest and the largest news-gathering organization. It is unique among agencies as a nonprofit cooperative. All of its income (the current budget runs over one million dollars a week) goes into news collection and dissemination. Since its founding in 1848, and more especially since the AP assumed its modern form around 1900, it has been a major influence in U.S. journalism.

AP's ranks have included many of the best writers, reporters, editors and news photographers in the profession, with twenty-five Pulitzer Prizes to show for it. Born in the infancy of telegraphy, the AP has pioneered in the application of new technology to news transmission, from the taps of the Morse code forward through the complex leased wire systems, teleprinters, instantaneous picture transmission (Wirephoto) to today's multiplying computer uses.

Rene J. Cappon. General News Editor of The Associated Press.

Equally important, the AP has been influential, by precept and example, in developing the principle of objective news. News written to inform, not to persuade or promote a cause, has been basic AP policy since its inception. Serving members of widely disparate political and editorial philosophy, the association could not adopt any particular view. It was something of an innovation in an era just beginning to emerge from the dark ages of press partisanship and highly colored news.

The AP was established by six New York newspapers as a method of reducing news gathering costs by a joint venture. The founders' original plan for the association was modest. It was to supply routine news, like shipping and market reports, while the six continued to compete among themselves on major stories.

But as the AP grew with the expansion of the United States press, the increasing membership took a less restrictive view. It was soon recognized that the AP could supply general and comprehensive news services that no paper alone could afford to maintain.

Today the AP performs a dual role. It is the news service of record, reporting global events as they occur, from wars to elections, from earthquakes to space flights. But it is also a service of news significance, providing the connective tissue between events, their background and meaning. The AP has shown in practice that neutrality in the news does not inhibit lively writing, interpretation, and investigative reporting—nor for that matter any of the most creative expressions of contemporary journalism.

So a day's news report may include matters of transient interest like a bus accident in Indiana and a demonstration in Detroit—and also an analysis of the ethical problems involved in organ transplants and a dissection of the causes of political violence. It may intrigue some readers with the latest word on Miss America, and others with a reflective, 5,000-word article on the quality of American life.

Diversity, then, is one characteristic of the AP service. Speed and comprehensiveness are others. A rather startling volume of copy—three million words a day—pours through the agency's network of teletype, cable and radio circuits that link more than 8,500 newspapers, radio and television stations in more than 100 countries. No network member is more than a minute away from an important news break.

Of course, not all of this immense news stream reaches any individual newspaper. Some of it is of interest only within a certain state, region, or country. Continuous editing judgment and selection on various control desks sort and channel the flow to the appropriate groups of members.

AP news is gathered and distributed by 3,300 employes deployed in 106 domestic and sixty foreign bureaus. Bureaus vary in size with their news responsibilities which are less extensive, say, in Pierre, South Dakota, than in Chicago—but the essentials of the work are the same.

Washington, covering the vastness of the Federal government and operating on the rim of a perpetual news volcano, is the largest domestic bureau with ninety newsmen. Each bureau covers its city and area. But a special strength of the AP lies in its cooperative structure. Under it, more than 1,260 daily newspaper members obligate themselves to make their local news available to the AP. Little of consequence can escape this vigilant network.

A portion of the news reported by the AP bureaus (whether it originates with the members or the bureau staffs) is of interest primarily within their own states and distributed within those boundaries. News of broader significance is sent on by the bureaus to the national wires.

This phase of the report is directed and supervised from AP headquarters in New York. The main line is the A wire; it carries the prime national and international news, interpretive and background articles, much news enterprise from AP staffers around the world, in-depth material for Sunday papers from AP Newsfeatures, and a selection of columns and features.

There are other national wires as well, for business and financial, sports and regional news. For smaller members with less space there is a single circuit combining all those branches with general news from the A in a condensed package. This wire, through a computer hookup, produces punched tape for direct use in newspaper typesetting machines. Tape of the full A wire report is similarly provided by a computer operation.

The news wires operate at sixty-six words per minute. Copy is sent by operators using teletype keyboards and is received the instant it is transmitted on printers in newspaper and broadcast newsrooms. But there are AP services with much higher transmission speeds: Stock market tables, certain texts, and sports copy during peak periods are sent at 1,050 words per minute. Computers are used in all these instances which exemplify the remarkable new communications vistas now opening up.

In charge of the general news report and the A wire is the General Desk in New York, manned around the clock by specially qualified editors and supervisors. Most bureaus can send their dispatches directly on the A and other wires, though often their copy is brought into New York on a collection wire to benefit from additional scrutiny before transmission on the A.

The General Desk decides which dispatches go on the A, in what sequence, and at what length. How many words is a story worth? This is a matter of professional news judgment and almost impossible to fix by any meaningful rule. A report on a presidential press conference or the death of a leading statesman will obviously require much more wordage than a routine political announcement.

News being relative, length will also depend on what other important events are happening that day. Space on the wire is always limited, and when major stories are breaking, secondary dispatches must be cut or discarded.

In addition to determining news priorities, the General Desk also scrutinizes the report closely for error, incompleteness and imbalance, ordering revisions or corrections where necessary. It will suggest the development of important angles, coordinate coverage of stories with related developments in several places and, in short, act both as traffic cop and central quality control.

The AP produces two complete news reports every twenty-four hours—one for morning papers and one for afternoon papers. A newspaper each day need concern itself only with the events up to its publication time. For the AP, the pulse never slackens; no sooner does one cycle near its end than it must go about the task of laying down the next cycle's report. Important stories that break in one cycle are, of course, carried over in the next; but AP writers strive to produce new material and a fresh approach for the second cycle's version.

A newspaper reporter faces a fixed and predictable deadline. But the AP is always on deadline. Somewhere in its far-flung membership, straddling all time zones, somebody is always nearing press time. A riot breaks out at 2 P.M. in a city with a morning newspaper. That paper can wait some hours until the complicated story jells before producing its story. But the AP must get the important developments as they occur, without delay, adding details as they come in, revising and updating as matters unfold. Otherwise important editions would be missed.

There is no basic difference between writing for the AP and

Editor Charles A. Grumich with AP Special Correspondent Saul Pett (left) and columnist Hal Boyle (right) at a desk in the AP offices in New York.

for newspapers, though the nature of AP operations accentuates proficiency in certain skills and techniques that may be less vital to other reporters.

Speed and accuracy are manifestly important. So is an economical, uncluttered style of writing. The AP reporter needs to have a quick grasp of the essentials of a story situation. He needs the ability to provide sufficient detail to reflect the drama, setting, and mood of events faithfully, but not to the point of prolixity.

Brevity is always a virtue, though it must not be at the expense of relevant facts and circumstances. The AP writer needs to construct his story lucidly and logically, with the important elements well to the front (though the old imperatives of cramming everything into the opening paragraph or two are, by and large, obsolete). Written in that manner, his story can be topped with new material without harming its structure, and editors can cut it, if need be, without difficulty.

While news conditions are often hectic, it must not be supposed that everything is produced under time pressure. In fact, there is another side to AP reporting: the kind that proceeds at a relatively leisurely pace, probes beneath the surface of events, explores neglected aspects of government or the economy or military affairs and examines in depth the great social currents, problems and controversies of our time.

This is the fertile area of news enterprise, equal in importance to spot news. And in this complex age, it is also often the area of the specialist.

The AP has a large corps of specialists—in science and medicine, space and environment, urban affairs and agriculture, fashion and aviation, diplomatic and military affairs, racial news and education, to mention some fields. It has an eleven-man team in Washington which specializes in investigative reporting, and a Living Today department in New York which reports especially for the younger generation.

Some of these specialists are stationed in Washington, New York, Cape Kennedy, Houston, Chicago and Los Angeles. Many devote all their time reporting nationally in their field. Others work on the bureau level and handle other duties as well.

They have a common denominator: They all started out as general reporters. Without ever letting go of the essentials of their craft, they moved into their specialties through their interest and initiative, capitalizing on background and experience, expanding their mastery through study and contacts.

And whether it's Alton Blakeslee assessing the latest development in cancer research, John M. Hightower dissecting the rationale behind the latest diplomatic moves, or Howard Benedict explaining the complexities of space technology, they write, as good reporters always do, for the lay reader rather than for other authorities.

Which is really what the AP is all about. A specialist writing on the national scene; a war correspondent reporting from Vietnam; a bureau newsman covering the politics of his state; a feature writer crisscrossing the country to assay the mood of the college generation—all have the same purpose: To report on human efforts and events with insight and detachment, giving readers a firm basis of facts by which to form their own judgments.

—RENE J. CAPPON,
General News Editor, the AP

OHIO UNIVERSITY LIBRARY

Please return this book as soon as y ve
finished with it. In order to avoid
be returned by the latest